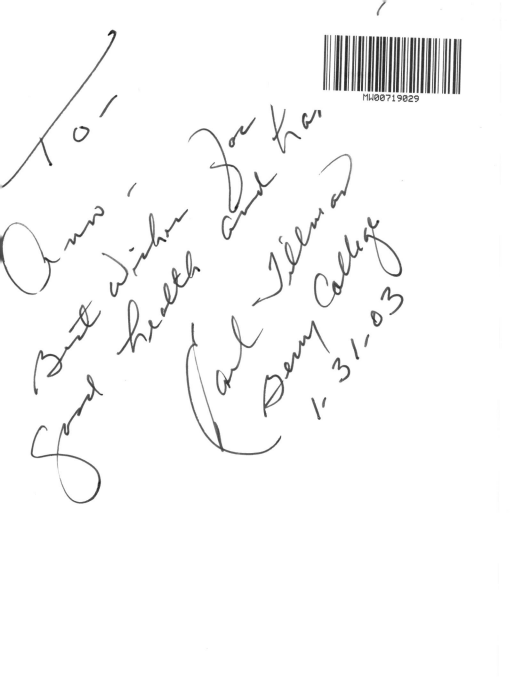

To:
Anne,
Best wishes for the
good health and

Carl Tillman
Berry College
1·31·03

How to Get a Raise or Promotion

Without Asking

. . . and How to Make the Most of What You Make

Earl Tillman
Wealth Communications
Rome, Georgia

Book design by Marc Bailey of Books International.
Jacket design by Bertram Gader.
Editing and project management by Ross West.

Publisher's Cataloging-in-Publication
(Provided by Quality Books, Inc.)

Tillman, Earl.
    How to get a raise or promotion without asking : and how to
make the most of what you make / Earl Tillman. —1st ed.
    p. cm.
    ISBN: 0-9659026-0-9
    1. Promotions. 2. Career development. 3. Negotiation in busi-
ness. 4. Finance, Personal.   I. Title.

HF5549.5.P7T55   1997   650.14
                                               QBI97–40818

First edition: October 1997

Printed in the United States of America.

10 9 8 7 6 5 4 3 2

Contents

Introduction

For many years I have felt there must be a better way to increase your paycheck rather than asking for a raise. I have watched people in clerical positions, entry-level positions, middle management, and senior management all struggle with the same basic problems—*how to get a raise or promotion without asking and how to make the most of what they make.*

Let's assume that at your company you are working with a reasonable supervisor, manager, vice president, and president. Doesn't it seem you should be able to progress in your paycheck and in your career based on your abilities? It would seem reasonable that as each of us makes a contribution to the organization we should receive reasonable compensation without the humiliation or fear of asking for a raise or promotion or wondering how to get one.

In fact, because of inflation we are worse off financially this year than last year if we do not increase our pay from the previous year. Furthermore, it's very important in the early years of our careers to make as much progress as possible to take advantage of the compounding effect of each raise. We fall behind if we don't.

So, you need a raise or promotion. I want to show you how to put yourself in the best position to receive one—with pride and dignity, and *without asking.* I also want to show you how to make the most of what you make. People fall behind if they don't learn how to do both of these things, with dignity and honesty.

Remember, no one of us is as smart as all of us. I've learned these lessons myself over a lifetime of experience in the workplace. I hope you'll take these ideas and suggestions that I have learned, combine them with your own, and start getting the raises or promotions you deserve.

Part I.

Here's Where to Start

1

How to Get a Raise or Promotion Without Asking

Let's get right to it with the basic steps you need to take if you want to get a raise or promotion without asking.

Step 1. Set Up an Interview

Call your immediate supervisor or write him or her a note. Ask for an appointment at your supervisor's convenience. Tell him or her you want to discuss a very important matter. Say that if possible you would like to meet for at least thirty minutes at a convenient location and time so that you will not be disturbed by the telephone or other distractions.

I can assure you the appointment will come sooner than you expect. I can just about assure you, too, that your supervisor will pressure you just a little about why you are requesting the private interview. Your supervisor may be thinking there is a problem.

Hold out for the interview. You might suggest that you feel the time will be equally important to your supervisor, to the company, and to you. If pressured, you might say you want to discuss your career goals. By the time the interview is held, your supervisor will probably have already shared with his or her immediate supervisor that you have requested a private meeting.

Stay positive as you wait. Lots of doubts may be going through your mind. Your supervisor's supervisor probably told him to find out whether there is a problem. They probably feel you're too good an employee to lose you.

Remember: No matter what your position in the company, you are a very important person. Some people feel they will be somebody when they are promoted from an entry-level, minimum wage position. Others feel they will be somebody when they become supervisor, manager, assistant vice president, vice president, or president. Of course, all of us want to progress in our careers. The fact is, though, you are *somebody* already. You don't have to wait. So do not accept negative thoughts from a co-worker, supervisor, manager, or someone even higher in the company.

If you have never been positive in your life, now is the time.

For many years I worked with young people at our church. The seed I tried to sow in these young people's minds is this: *You are somebody. You are God's creation, and God does not make junk!* That's so with you, too. So you have real value to your company or organization.

Step 2. The Day of the Interview

In other reviews and evaluations at your company, you probably have had butterflies. It's okay to have butterflies about this interview; just keep them flying in formation.

Today, the butterflies are probably in the stomach of your supervisor, too, because your supervisor does not know what you want. Be prepared, and have a checklist. (Don't be too surprised if your supervisor's immediate supervisor shows up also.)

I have made thousands of takeoffs and landings as a pilot. Each time, I have used a detailed checklist. The best pilots in the best airplanes always use a checklist. So prepare, and use a checklist to be sure you don't miss anything you want to discuss.

The moment of truth is here. The supervisor asks you, "What did you want to discuss with me?"

You reply, "Thank you for granting me this special time with you. I have several items I would like to discuss with you. I like my job. I like you as supervisor." (Of course, you might have to really be positive here. Several surveys reveal that many people do not really like their supervisor. We will discuss more about this later.) You continue, "I also like the company."

At this moment, the supervisor's heart has stopped pounding because he or she probably came to the interview expecting a big problem. The supervisor was probably thinking, "If there's a problem, we'll fix it." Why? The supervisor's manager probably said, "We do not want the expense of training another person for that position. Find out what the problem is, and get back with me."

So in the first ten seconds of the interview, you have already made the supervisor very happy because of the good news. There is no problem.

Now, tell your supervisor, "I do have a checklist I'd like to review with you. After we've reviewed it, we can talk again at your convenience." This is the only meeting you probably will need to request. Your supervisor will likely request the next meeting.

Here's the checklist. Make a copy for yourself and your supervisor.

- WHAT IS OUR COMPANY'S OBJECTIVE?

- HOW CAN I HELP ACHIEVE THIS OBJECTIVE?

- WHAT IS YOUR GOAL OR OBJECTIVE FOR THE COMPANY?

- HOW CAN I HELP YOU ACHIEVE YOUR GOAL?

- HOW CAN I CHANGE TO HELP YOU AND THE COMPANY REACH THESE OBJECTIVES?

- DO YOU FEEL I NEED TO TAKE ADDITIONAL TRAINING TO HELP YOU AND THE COMPANY ACHIEVE ITS OBJECTIVES?

- DO I NEED TO DRESS OR ACT DIFFERENTLY TO PROJECT THE PROPER IMAGE OF THE COMPANY?

You get the idea. Add to your checklist to fit your own situation.

Now is the time to be a little modest, but still positive. Speak up and say, "The last item I want to discuss with you is promotions and raises. I want to keep my mind on helping you and the company achieve our goals and objectives. I do not want to be drained mentally, wondering about my future. I know that if I can help you and the company achieve your goals, then I will achieve my goal. You take care of my promotions and pay raises, and I'll take care of your work."

Step 3. After the Interview

One of the first actions you need to take after the interview is to write the supervisor a note. In the note, thank the supervisor for the interview and say, "It's great working for and with you." Say also that you look forward to helping to achieve your supervisor's goals and the company's goals.

When you take this approach, you must stick to your promise. You must mean what you say, and say what you mean. If you talk the talk, you've got to walk the walk. Basically the message is, if you say you will do something, then do it. Your supervisor will know very soon whether you are for real. Are you really interested in the goals of your immediate supervisor, and are you really interested in the company's goals and objectives? If so, your supervisor will know it, and it will pay great dividends for you.

Your only follow-up will be in passing in the hall, meeting at the water fountain, or seeing each other at sporting events or social functions. Always be in a hurry unless the supervisor wants to talk. With a little smile and a near whisper, ask, "How am I doing?" You'll probably get an "at-a-boy" or "at-a-girl." "Keep up the good work," the supervisor will say, "and let's get together Tuesday at nine o'clock or Wednesday at lunch to discuss an idea."

Guess what? If your immediate supervisor has the qualities necessary to move up the ladder, your efforts will get him or her promoted. Whom do you think he or she will recommend to fill the vacancy? The person the supervisor trained and taught. We love mentors and love to be mentors.

What do you think most supervisors, managers, vice-presidents, and presidents brag about to their peers at conventions? You're right. They brag about the people they have promoted, developed, and guided up the ladder. If management people are worth their salt, they take pride in the people they develop, just as a mother and father do in their children's growth and development. This is true with teachers and coaches, too. They glory in the success of the young men and women they coach or teach. They have pride and satisfaction in their students' achievements.

Recently I observed with pride a couple of very successful people I had taught to fly an airplane. In my mind, I could see them when they did not know a rudder from an aileron. Now, each take-off and landing is as perfect as that of an old pro. They can command the skies and travel quickly and safely wherever they want to fly.

I've also had the opportunity to teach and coach many administrators, salespersons, and managers. My great pride has been in their success. Your supervisor will feel the same about you. You, too, will have pride in the people you help climb the ladder of success.

RAISE TIME—HAPPY OR SAD?

One person I know became worried and troubled every review time when the possibility of a raise in salary was being considered. The raise received was generally not what was expected. On the other hand, many of us have heard squeals of excitement or received such a positive and dignified handshake from the person who just had a positive annual review that we knew it had gone well.

All of us feel sad for people who are not progressing in their paycheck or position. We are happy for those who seem to hit every rung on the success ladder. Both of these observations become even more important when it is *us*. That's why this book is devoted to helping you get a raise or promotion without asking. We will include now and then a human interest story of a friend, co-worker, associate, or maybe a personal experience. I hope you also will receive a chuckle or two and realize the importance of keeping some humor in your life.

Right up front, I want to give you some "meat and potatoes," some essentials for helping you make review time happy, not sad. This first one might come as a big surprise to some. It's this: *You will not make it to the top by yourself.* What the poet said is true: "No man is an island." That goes for all of us. We need other people to help us be successful. Here are some other important ingredients:

- EDUCATION: GREAT STUFF. WE NEED AS MUCH AS WE CAN GET.

- PERSONALITY: GREAT TO HAVE—IF IT'S NOT TOO OVER-POWERING AND IF IT DOES NOT OVERSHADOW YOUR IMMEDIATE SUPERVISOR.

- TEMPER: SOME IS GOOD—WHEN USED AT THE PROPER TIME, IF IT SHOWS YOU ARE NOT A PUSHOVER, IF IT IS USED FOR YOUR BEST INTEREST AND THE BEST INTEREST OF YOUR SUPERVISOR, AND IF IT HELPS PROMOTE THE CORPORATE GOALS AND OBJECTIVES.

- LOYALTY: BE SURE AND SHOW COMPANY LOYALTY EARLY IN YOUR CAREER. LOYALTY IS VERY IMPORTANT TO YOUR SUPERVISOR AND YOUR COMPANY OR ORGANIZATION. NOTHING WILL DESTROY A RELATIONSHIP QUICKER THAN A LACK OF LOYALTY.

- TRUST: YOUR SUPERVISOR TRUSTS YOU TO TAKE CARE OF

THE COMPANY'S BUSINESS JUST AS IF THE BUSINESS BELONGED TO YOU. IT IS VERY IMPORTANT FOR YOUR SUPERVISOR TO KNOW THE COMPANY CAN TRUST YOU WITH CONFIDENTIAL INFORMATION. IN ANY RELATIONSHIP, WHEN THE TRUST LEVEL GOES UP THE TENSION LEVEL GOES DOWN.

• INTEREST: NOT JUST THE KIND WE GET AT THE BANK, BUT AN INTEREST IN THE PROGRESS OF YOUR SUPERVISOR'S SUCCESS AND AN INTEREST IN THE OVERALL OBJECTIVES OF THE COMPANY.

Giant Steps Toward Getting a Raise or Promotion

You feel you have earned a raise or promotion. You have worked hard; you have been loyal to the company, to the school system, to the military, or to whatever organization for which you work. You are loyal, and you support all levels of management. You believe in the product or service your organization provides to the consumer.

With all of these points in your favor, you feel your supervisor, company management, and other decision makers who control your paycheck should recognize your ability and contributions to the organization. You wonder why you should have to ask for a raise or promotion. Congratulations on your decision to read this book. It's intended to help you never to have to feel guilty, intimidated, or bashful about receiving what you feel you deserve—a raise or promotion.

In some cases, you will use the step-by-step methods the book suggests. In other cases, you will say to yourself, "I don't feel comfortable doing it the way the book suggested." In that case, these suggestions will cause you to design an action plan for your career that you like even better.

I've observed promotions and raises in my own life for many years and in the lives of many friends and co-workers. Early in my career I observed a person who was a loyal and dedicated employee. All year this employee was loyal, productive and happy. Then it was time for the annual review. Each time the supervisor brought the decision about the employee's annual review from top management, the employee would become sad and withdrawn.

Something about this did not seem right to me. For the most part, the employee was very happy at work. So why the sadness? Did the employee expect more? Did the employee need a different assignment? Did anyone ever talk with the employee about what actions needed to be taken to earn more and grow with the company? Did not a longtime employee deserve more than a slightly above entry-level employee? Did the supervisor sell top management on the employee's talent and worth? Did the employee sell the company and the supervisor on the contribution the employee was making? Or was the employee just taken for granted?

Within a couple of days after the review, this employee would never mention the results of the review. The sadness was gone and productivity seemed again to be at a high level.

I finally learned the reason for the employee's behavior. I learned the employee just would not go through the humiliation of asking for a raise. The supervisor knew the employee would not quit. So the employee got little increase in salary.

This employee was no different from most of us. The employee wanted nice clothes, a safe car, and a comfortable home, just like most of us. But the employee would not take the steps needed to get the deserved raise.

Look around and you will find most of us want about the same sorts of things for ourselves and our families. Most of us want to earn what we perceive as fair return for the contribution we make to the company or organization we serve. We need to learn how to take the steps to get that return.

The prime motivation for this book is to help you achieve a high level of the "good life" for you and your family. The book is aimed at helping you get paid well for what you do.

You have studied and prepared yourself by graduating from a trade school, high school, college, university, business school, or professional school. You could be at an entry-level position, in middle management, or quite a few years into your career. Whatever your education and experience, you now find yourself on someone's payroll in the business world. This book focuses first on people in this situation, whether they receive a salary, hourly wages, or commissions. The book also provides help to people who own their own business or are in a professional partnership.

I don't want to forget, of course, the person who is in what I refer to as a "high calling," in which service to others comes from motivations higher than financial reward. When the final bell has rung, this "high calling" might very well exceed all others. This area, however, is not the emphasis of this book. It *is* up to us, however, to help those who have accepted that special call.

Let's first be clear on our understanding of work itself. Here's an important understanding about work: *All work is honorable as long as it legal and ethical.*

Our society holds in high esteem a person who will put in a good day's work for a good day's pay. Observe people at a civic club or church; on a bus, train, or airplane; at a party; or wherever people meet for the first time. The first question is usually this one: "What do you do?" Most folks will answer that question by describing their occupation—truck driver, airplane pilot, homemaker, college president, computer programmer, teacher, office manager, sales person, military, or a thousand other ways people earn a living.

All of these people have at least one thing in common. They want to be compensated fairly for what they do. You do, too. So it is time for you to take charge of your paycheck and take advantage of opportunities for your career. This can be done by having a "master plan" for your career and working closely with your supervisor and your company.

Find a Job You Like

Your first step must be to try to find a job you like and enjoy, if at all possible. If you can work in a job that you enjoy so much that the compensation does not matter, you can just about be assured that you will do so well that the compensation will be at a high level.

Have Self-Confidence

Second, it will boost your confidence if you will realize that the company or organization probably needs you as much as you need them. You likely would not have gotten the job in the first place or still have it if that assumption were not correct.

I've had the honor of working with young people and have found that many lack self-confidence. They do not see themselves in a positive light. Surveys have revealed that some of the great beauties do not see themselves as beautiful and some of the brightest young people do not see themselves as very smart.

We do not like to see people boasting of their beauty or intellect. However, we do want them to have the self-confidence to accept a challenge and not be afraid to take a risk in a business or a profession. Usually the greater the risk, the greater the reward. Most of us who have been around for some time admire the people who accentuate the positive and eliminate the negative, and who are willing to take a risk by investing their money or time in a career or project.

Remember: You are important, and you are God's creation. Therefore, it's reasonable for you to think positively about yourself. If you do, others will think positively of you. If you treat others in a business-like, professional manner, others will treat you the same way. If you expect fair payment for your work or service, you are much closer to receiving it than if you have negative expectations.

Have the Right Attitude Toward the Company

Third, you need the right attitude toward the company or

organization for which you work. If you belittle the company, you should either stop that practice or find somewhere else to work. It's not worth it to spend a lifetime working for an organization while hating the management, disliking the product the com-pany produces, or feeling the organization is a "rip-off" to the public.

Remember, there are many management styles. Often you will learn as much from the styles you do not like as those you do like. When you enter management or a leadership position, remember the things your previous supervisor or manager did. Do the things you liked and don't do the things you disliked. You will have gained from both—the things you disliked as well as the things you liked.

Have the Right Attitude Toward Your Co-workers

Fourth, you need the right attitude toward your fellow workers. Most projects are completed and goals reached through teamwork. We've seen so many times the importance of team-work, whether it was in putting a person on the moon, getting a product to the market on time, meeting a quarterly sales objec-tive, or hitting the bottom line objectives.

Many people have lost good jobs or failed to get a raise or pro-motion, not because of a lack of education or know-how, but because of their inability or unwillingness to work with people as teammates. They would not or could not get along with their supervisor, manager, or co-worker.

There are times to push forward to achieve a goal your way and times to back off. The military calls the latter operation a "strategic withdrawal." It does not help your cause to win a battle and lose the war. You want to win the war and thus to make what-ever adjustments are necessary to win. To change the image to football, sometimes you need to run full speed straight ahead, accepting whatever blocks you can get, and other times the end-around might be the best play.

Your supervisor may not be right, but your supervisor is still the supervisor. You will get excellent marks by pushing your point, but don't push yourself into a corner. Think carefully before giving an ultimatum to the people who hold the power, especially if they have influence over your paycheck or advancement within the organization.

General Douglas MacArthur had to learn this lesson in his relationship with President Harry Truman. General MacArthur had a strong opinion on how to stop aggression, but President Truman did not want to risk a World War III. More than forty-five years later, people still debate who was right. Whatever the case, the point to notice here is that President Truman, once an army captain but then the President of the United States, was the Commander-in-Chief and had the final say. So know when to push forward with your ideas and know when to back off.

Know the Company's Immediate Goal

Fifth, try to have a general idea—and a specific idea is better—of what your company is trying to achieve. Companies and organizations go through cycles. Sometimes the goal is full speed ahead for production and expansion. Sometimes the goal is conservation, belt-tightening, and downsizing. In addition to doing the best job you can in your assignment, make a special effort to know as much as possible about the organization's immediate goals as well as its long-term goals.

You may have the best idea in town for expansion, new products, or updating to the latest computers. At the right point in the company's cycle, that idea might assure you a promotion or a very good raise. However, if the current thrust is conservation, belt-tightening, or downsizing, you will help yourself more if you will present an idea that will save the company millions of dollars and get the bottom line to an all-time high.

Know Your Supervisor's Goal

Now that you know the company or organization's goal, make a special effort to know your supervisor's goal. Meet with the supervisor, and ask how you can help the supervisor reach his or her career goal.

Too, if you have an idea or suggestion that will help the company achieve an objective, get your supervisor involved in the project as early as possible. Don't be afraid to make a suggestion. If your idea or suggestion will make or save the organization lots of money, then push full-speed ahead, but always keep your supervisor aware of the progress. Eliminate as many surprises as possible for your supervisor.

As you seek approval from your supervisor, sometimes you will want general approval but not an opinion on every detail of the project. In fact, if you feel keenly about one aspect of a project, give your supervisor a progress report, but do not seek your supervisor's final opinion on that detail. If your supervisor's opinion is different from yours and you try to adjust the project to please the supervisor, it may frustrate you and cause the final results to be much different from your plan. Remember, you have been assigned the project because of your knowledge, experience, and creativity.

Be sure to rely on and call on your supervisor when help is needed, though. Your supervisor will help you present the money-making or money-saving idea to top management.

People sometimes become impatient with the slow pace of their supervisor. They may decide to bypass the immediate supervisor and push forward on their own fast-track plans. Such an action is generally fatal to a person's job with that company or organization. Always remember that your supervisor also has a supervisor and that he or she knows what you both are doing.

Ask Your Supervisor for Help in Planning Your Career

After you have seen your supervisor's career plan and have an understanding of how you can help with his or her career, you have completed an important step. The next step is to ask your supervisor to help you design a plan for your own career.

4

The Big Mess-Up

Recently I spoke to a senior manager who reminded me of an important piece of advice about getting pay raises and promotions. Knowing that many pay raises are given in January, he commented: "Don't mess up in December."

The reason is obvious. The people in the position to increase your paycheck are most prone to take positive or negative action based on your current activity rather than the total year of work.

That makes timing important. Some folks play golf or tennis. Some like to cook. Others like to work in the yard, do woodwork, needlepoint, or embroider. Many wives will say their husbands watch too many ball games. One wife told her husband, "All you think about is sports! You love football more than me." To which he replied, "Maybe, but I love you more than basketball." Timing is important.

I have been flying airplanes for many years. Over the years I've earned a private pilot's license and commercial pilot license. I've added to these an instrument rating and an instructor's rating. In each flying lesson we receive eight to ten "at-a-boy/girl" affirmations and one "ah, shucks" criticism. (One "ah, shucks" will wipe out fifteen "at-a-boy/girl" affirmations.)

This realization caused me to believe that the senior manager was correct and that we should incorporate this reality into our plan for getting a raise or promotion. Because reviewers tend to base annual raises on the latest things you've done instead of the total review period, keep a success notebook. Make a list of the things you see other successful people doing, try to do those things, and keep a record of them in your success notebook. Also, keep an affirmation file of letters, cards, comments, and promotions related to your work in civic organizations, church organizations, and professional associations. Read these when you get discouraged. Most of all, be sure you keep a record of your work accomplishments and record these accomplishments in your personnel file. If you do "mess up in December," you can point to your accomplishments earlier in the year.

Prepare for the Annual Review

The annual review can be a horror story or a learning experience for both the employee and the supervisor. Many people expect luck to take care of them in the review. However, most will agree that the harder we work the better luck we have. The reward will come, not so much from the work itself but rather from the results that work produced. It's better to prepare than to depend on luck.

Often a raise is based on the overall success of the company for that year. So, once again, try to get a good understanding of the company's overall objectives for that year. Do your part and let it be known that you are making a special effort to achieve the company's objectives.

Raises come in all forms. Some are called merit raises; others, seniority, time in service, inflation, and the list goes on. It does not much matter what you call it. What matters is the amount and frequency of the raise, as reflected in your W-2 form or form 1099 at the end of the year.

Some top executives and professionals reach the point in their careers where they just do not want any more money. They do want to be rewarded for their work, however. They prefer to be rewarded with stock options, new company cars, a company jet, and unlimited expense accounts.

On the other hand, most of us don't fit in that category. If we are answering the telephone, looking at a computer screen, or making middle management decisions all day, the current paycheck is very important to us. Paying the bills that week or month is at the top of our list. The extra perks for the so-called "good life" likely are only in the back of our mind for some time in the future. For today, we just want to get through the review successfully so maybe this year we can get the house painted, get new tires for the car, maybe even trade for a better car, get braces on our daughter's teeth, and send our son to baseball camp.

These kinds of needs make the review and raise very important to us. Just remember: $10.00 per week equals $20,800 over a forty-year career.

So we see what the company is doing. We want to be part of that success. We want to know how we can make things happen.

Since my army aviation days, I have continued to fly general aviation airplanes. These airplanes carry four-to-six people and fly 150 to 200 miles per hour. They are excellent business transportation.

I teach a few people to fly each year. Safety is the primary goal, and the safety record of these planes and their pilots continues to improve. As an instructor check pilot, when I give annual and biannual flight reviews (BFR), I no longer look at these reviews as testing but rather as teaching. In these reviews, I have the opportunity to help the pilot become a safer pilot.

To accomplish this goal, all pilots use a very detailed check list. The pilot must achieve certain standards on the annual review. Additional training may be required. My responsibility in the review is to be sure the pilot does not have a weakness that could hurt the pilot or others. We use a very detailed checklist and review form in the pilot review.

At your company, the annual review form may be very detailed or very simple. Most will include items such as the following:

- WORKS WELL WITH OTHERS

- COMPLETES PROJECTS ON TIME

- IS A TEAM PLAYER

- UNDERSTANDS THE ORGANIZATION'S OBJECTIVES

- MAKES SERVICE A HIGH PRIORITY

- CONSIDERS QUALITY VERY IMPORTANT

- IS PRESENT AND ON TIME

- CONTINUES TO IMPROVE TECHNICAL JOB SKILLS

- CONTINUES TO IMPROVE PEOPLE SKILLS

- IS INVOLVED IN NIGHT SCHOOL, MANAGEMENT TRAINING, OR POST-GRADUATE STUDIES

In some ways, the annual review at work has the same sort of function as the pilot review or even our annual health examination. With our annual health examination, parts of it are not much fun, but those parts have proven to save many lives. Most of us are looking for better ways to keep safe and healthy, but we may spend very little time reviewing our financial and work well-being. We just leave it to our employer and hope for the best. This could be really hazardous for our financial health.

Give your attention to getting ready for the annual review. Learn from it, and be even more prepared the next time.

6

How to negotiate a Bigger Raise

The main theme of this book is on how to get a raise or promotion without asking. The idea is to avoid the intimidation and fear of facing up to the Big People on the 42nd floor or in the big corner office. However, while this is a goal of millions of people in the workplace, there are a great many who like a good mental scrap. To be truthful, I like the idea myself.

For much of your career, while paying for a car, educating children, buying groceries, and making house payments, maybe you did not feel you had the luxury of standing up for what you felt was fair compensation. However, if you have a little scrap in your bones and are willing to do something, then you may want to try negotiating. You might surprise yourself.

Negotiation is not for everyone, though. Some of us may feel we are pretty good negotiators when it comes to trading cars. However, one recent survey revealed that many Americans would rather have a root canal than negotiate for an automobile.

Did you ever wonder why movie stars and sports figures have agents? why manufacturing companies have agents to sell and market their product? why governments have negotiators to negotiate terms of war and peace? or why thousands have joined unions to have someone negotiate their contract for them? They feel someone else can better represent them than they can represent themselves. Most of the time they are correct in this belief.

But let's suppose you want to negotiate a bigger raise. You no longer want to wait for the "automatic" raise. What I'm going to suggest about negotiating is for any level of the workplace. It could be for the entry-level position or for the CEO. Let's split the difference and use middle management as the example.

To begin with, you need a plan. Here are some things to consider:

- WHY DO YOU DESERVE A BIGGER PAYCHECK?

- WHAT IS YOUR VALUE TO THE COMPANY?

- WHAT ARE YOU WILLING TO ACCEPT IN SALARY, FRINGE BENE-FITS, ETC.?

- WHAT ARE THE SALARY LEVELS IN YOUR COMPANY?

- HOW WILL YOUR BOSS REACT TO YOUR REQUEST?

- WHAT WILL BE YOUR STRATEGY FOR NEGOTIATING YOUR RAISE?

Many middle managers are no longer willing to see their CEO get an average 30% per annum increase and see the production line worker receive 5%. Middle managers feel there must be a good fit between the two extremes. They are no longer happy with a seniority plaque. They want recognition in the billfold. They want fairness from their corporation.

A ten-year study revealed that the CEO and the production workers got their raises. However, when middle managers faced the CEO, they heard, "It was just not a good year." So their raises did not keep up with inflation.

Most airline magazines carry an ad for a book or seminar that says, "You can negotiate anything." Some will say that the best money a person can make comes when negotiating his or her own raise.

Much has been written about "win-win" as a method. Win-win occurs when both parties to a transaction are happy with the transaction. Both sides win. So, negotiation is considered a success when both parties profit.

You can be an excellent negotiator, but you need a few skills in your corner. You might not have all the skills in your early man-

agement career, but you will gain more and more as you negotiate. You will need to know and have a feel for the following:

- YOUR VALUE TO THE COMPANY OR ORGANIZATION

- HOW TO BE IN CHARGE BUT LET THE BIG BOSS STILL BE THE
COMMANDER

- AN ABILITY TO COMMUNICATE AND READ THE BOSS'S EXPRES-
SIONS BETTER THAN A MISSISSIPPI RIVERBOAT GAMBLER

- WHEN A "NO" IS A "MAYBE"

- LISTENING SKILLS

- YOUR SUPERVISOR'S NEEDS AND HOW YOU WILL FILL THOSE
NEEDS

To be a good negotiator will require desire, aspiration, skill,
and belief in yourself. Also throw in a good dose of self-confidence. You must have the ability to plan, think under stress, smile,
grin, listen, understand the other person's position, stick with the
facts, be honest, and "never let 'em see you sweat."

A middle-manager friend of mine has an excellent opportunity
to become vice president and manager of his department. He
thought he should have received the promotion a few years ago
when another person received the top position and he was the
assistant. The manager of the department has accepted a position
with another company, and the position my friend wants is available. Both he and his wife believe he is qualified for the position.
Since they are both friends of mine, they have spoken with me
about the opportunity. I encouraged him a few years back not to
leave his company and to be patient. I believe he will get the position if he will stick to the rules of negotiation.

The manager's wife told me her husband had a list of things he
would discuss with the president this week and if he did not get the

promotion he would be "out of there." She said his ego would not allow him to remain with the company if he did not receive the top vice president position of the department. Immediately I thought of how Chuck Yeager, the test pilot, said he managed to stay alive. "Leave yourself a way out," he said. The point here is, if you already have your mind made up, there is no room for negotiation.

If you want to have some fun, advertise your car in the paper for sale. Maybe it's time for you to buy a new car, a later model, or you just enjoy negotiating. Look in the blue book, black book, or any number of publications. Also, get three appraisals of your car's value. Ask for the wholesale price, the loan value, and the retail value. You are now quite knowledgeable about the value. You probably know more about that one car based on the appraisal, check by a good mechanic, and the book value, than any other one person.

Put the ad in your local newspaper and wait for the calls. Put the price in the paper, too; that will save you at lot of time. You will find that there are some "tire kickers," who don't buy but just kick the tires. They are like one couple I've known for twenty-five years who look at houses every Sunday afternoon and are still renting. The style or price is never quite right.

Soon the phone will ring and the person will say, "I am calling about your car you have for sale." Thank the person for the call and invite him or her to come see the car. Without seeing the car or knowing the value, the person will ask, "What is your 'bottom dollar' for the car?"

You very politely tell the caller the price was published in the paper and you would be happy to show the car. The caller will then tell you he has cash, and he is not "wishie washie." His word is his bond, he continues, and he will do exactly what he says he will do. Then the caller will tell you he is not a "haggler."

The caller wants to know your "bottom dollar. What is the least you will take?"

You reply, "What is the least you will give?"

The caller breaks in again and says one more time, "What is your bottom dollar? What is the least you will take?"

You reply, "What is the least you will give?"

By this time, he is calling his wife. "Martha, you are not going to believe this. I've got a 'feller' on the phone I'm talking to about his car. I'm asking what is the least he will take and he is asking what is the least I will give."

This sort of interchange happens more often than we might think. The value has nothing to do with the price when a person only negotiates price. Chances are he will come over and buy the car because he thinks he just met the worst negotiator he has ever called.

As you prepare to negotiate in your annual salary review, ask yourself a few questions about your value to the company.

- WHAT CAN YOU DO TO IMPROVE YOUR VALUE TO THE COMPANY?

- WHAT ABOUT YOUR PROFESSIONAL EDUCATION?

- HOW ARE YOU DOING ON YOUR CAREER SALARY GOAL?

- DO YOU FIT THE COMPANY? DOES THE COMPANY FIT YOU?

- WHAT ARE YOUR GOALS AND OBJECTIVES?

- WHAT ARE YOUR PLUSSES AND MINUSES?

- ARE THE RESULTS OF YOUR WORK MORE THAN EXPECTED?

- WILL YOU "WALK" IF YOU DON'T GET THE RAISE?

After you get clear on your answers to these questions plus any others you want to add to the list, you are ready for the review.

Remember, your boss was a person, a real human being, before he or she got the title of CEO, President, Vice President, COF, CFO, HMO, IMO, CLU, CFI, or whatever the title. The boss also has desires, goals, and aspirations. The boss has one kind of pressure, and you may have another. So, make the following a part of your check list. If pilots use a check list for safety, a check list for negotiating your pay raise is a great idea.

- THE BOSS KNOWS YOU. DO YOU KNOW THE BOSS? What about his or her education? If the boss started in the stockroom and you came from the MBA classroom, you need to know. he or she may want his or her daughter to get an MBA and not start in the stockroom. what about civic organizations, sports, hobbies, or marital status? I don't play golf, but I have many friends who do. Just a spark of interest about your visit to Augusta for the Masters may open a wide door in getting to know the boss.

- BE POSITIVE. The board chairman just asked for a 10% decrease in expenses and you are asking for a 15% pay raise. Your request is reasonable because you have suggested a way to decrease expenses by 15% and increase production by 30%.

- BE CALM.

- DON'T PAINT THE BOSS IN A CORNER.

- SHOW WHAT THE COMPANY HAS DONE SINCE YOUR EMPLOY-MENT. A WELL-PREPARED GRAPH IS A WINNER.

- DON'T WANDER. STICK TO THE SUBJECT—YOUR PAY RAISE OR PROMOTION.

- YOU DON'T HAVE TO KNOW ALL THE ANSWERS. THINK, THEN SPEAK. WHEN ANSWERING QUESTIONS, REMEMBER THAT A FEW MOMENTS OF SILENCE BEFORE ANSWERING MAY BE GOLDEN.

- POWER—BE CAREFUL NOT TO COME ON TOO STRONG, BUT DO NOT BE BULLIED BY YOUR BOSS'S POSITION. A spreadsheet, graph, or whatever you can use to get the boss to move from behind the big desk to another chair or to a conference table to look at it is a good move. this helps get the conversation on equal footing.

- POWER, POSITION, MONEY—SOMEONE ONCE SAID THAT YOU CANNOT INTIMIDATE THE POWERFUL AND THE RICH. So, if the boss is the company owner's son, daughter, son-in-law, daughter-in-law, or other family member or close friend, never give the impression you know how they got where they are in the organization, unless you already have your resumé approved with another organization. Most of the major corporations in the nineteenth and twentieth centuries were owned and operated by family members. So, if you want to go into the twenty-first century with a company that is closely held, then avoid discussion of how your boss advanced to a high position so quickly unless you want to have the boss give you a company history lesson.

- RAISE, PROMOTION—WE ARE USING THESE TWO WORDS TOGETHER FOR MUCH OF OUR DISCUSSION IN THIS BOOK. HOWEVER, WE KNOW IN MOST CAREERS THERE ARE MORE OPPORTUNITIES FOR A PAY RAISE THAN FOR A PROMOTION. TRY TO GET BOTH OF THEM IF YOU CAN, THOUGH.

- IF YOU HAVE REAL "GUTS," FEEL KEENLY ABOUT YOUR FUTURE, SEE THERE IS NO PAY RAISE AND NO PROMOTION AHEAD, AND FEEL YOU ARE AT A DEAD END, THEN ASK FOR A TRANSFER OR BE WILLING TO RESIGN. Make this decision with your mind and not with your feelings. Consider all the facts, and remember you cannot intimidate the rich and powerful. *P.S. But don't be afraid. negotiate with confidence. One more P.S. Know the job market for your skills before you take this last step.*

COMMISSIONS

One of the quickest ways to get a big pay raise is to quit your forty-hour-per-week or salary job and go to work on commission. This could be the greatest risk you could take. You have often heard "the greater the risk, the greater the reward." Sometimes that statement is true, and sometime it's not.

If you believe in yourself and believe in your product, you have just made a giant step if you begin selling on commission. However, your belief may be short-lived if there is not a market for your product.

Many very successful people will tell you what a great salesperson they were the first year of selling. They sold their furniture, they sold their house, and they sold their car!

There are plenty of examples, though, of people quitting dead-end jobs, even though the salary was good, for an opportunity to do much better. Real estate, insurance, automobiles, computers, heavy equipment, and textiles are just a few areas where both men and women have greatly increased their income by selling on commission.

But before you switch to commission selling, ask questions, see where the needs are, and look at the top and low end of earnings. Sometimes the low side of the commission job will be better than the high side of the administrative position, so don't get discouraged. Get as many facts as you can before you turn in your resignation.

If you make a decision to work for commission, burn the bridge and don't look back. Be the best you can be.

8

Work for the Company Bonus

Sometimes the most you can expect in a cost-of-living pay raise will be three or four percent. Incentive pay must be earned every year, but it may be seven to eight percent of base salary. If your company will continue to raise your base pay through a cost-of-living raise and also give you an incentive bonus based on performance, you will be "cooking on the front burner."

You may be working for the biggest possible bonus, but you are also setting yourself up for a promotion. These incentives will cause you to work at a high level of your potential. When you are working at peak performance, you are finding problems that need to be fixed or opportunities for the organization that will improve the bottom line.

This is exactly what happened to General Dwight D. Eisenhower. The top military people in Washington asked him to complete a plan to free Europe and stop the Nazi aggression led by Adolf Hitler in World War II. The Joint Chiefs of Staff and President Roosevelt liked the plan so well that they asked General Eisenhower to implement the plan. The rest really is history.

Not only did General Eisenhower lead the American troops, but he was selected to command all allied forces in Europe. His plan won approval by our nation's top military people and President Roosevelt and also was supported by our allied commanders. General Eisenhower instilled a winning spirit in our troops, our allies' troops, and the officers who led them. This winning spirit stopped the Nazi aggression and defeated Adolf Hitler.

General Eisenhower found a place in the hearts of the

American people and freedom-loving people around the world. Several months ago I toured the D-Day Museum and Overlord Embroidery at Portsmouth, England, and I was grateful once again for General Eisenhower and his plan.

Your plan may not save the free world, but it could save your company or organization. When it does, the pay raise or promotion will be way down the list compared to your satisfaction of having devised a plan of action and then implemented that plan. The good news is that you likely will not have to ask for the pay raise or promotion.

LEAVE YOURSELF A WAY OUT

General Charles "Chuck" Yeager, the famous test pilot, was the first pilot to break the sound barrier. He is credited with helping to move us from the Jet Age to the Space Age. The aircraft companies and the military were able to see exactly what a plane would or would not do after being tested by Chuck Yeager. He pushed the aircraft to the limit, meaning more than would be expected in normal operation. Those tests undoubtedly saved many lives and millions of dollars for the companies and for taxpayers.

During his career, General Yeager had several accidents. He always survived the crash or malfunction of the aircraft, though. Someone once asked him how he managed to survive all the tests and some serious accidents. He indicated that he always left himself a way out. He considered all the options and knew when to stay with the aircraft and when to "bail out."

If things are not going the way you feel they should be going in your career, don't "bail out" at the first sign of danger. Look at your options. Now might be the time for you to put the creative juices to work. Now might be the time to take your supervisor an idea that will correct a problem. This suggestion might very well improve the bottom line, increase productivity, or streamline the department.

So many people will go steaming into management's office with an ultimatum. They want certain actions to be taken immediately or they are "bailing out." Often the reply will be, "Be careful not to let the door hit your backside too hard when you leave."

A much better approach might be asking a question related to an idea you have for making improvements. For example, a person might ask his or her manager, "Do you think the accounting department should be moved across the hall from the investment department? That might help the accounting department coordinate their activities with the investment department a little better. The investment department seems to have a real sense of urgency about getting the numbers as quickly as possible. Quick investment of company dollars will make a big difference in our bottom line."

The manager's reply might be, "Let me think about your question. It sounds like a good idea."

You might be in building 2-B, on the 4th floor. Often the elevator does not work, and the building is hot in the summer and cold in the winter. You have had it up to your limit, and the problem with the building is the last straw. It seems management just cannot see the obvious. You begin to think it's time to "bail out" if the problem is not corrected immediately.

Just last evening, though, the manager thought of your question. First thing the next day he talks to the big folks on the 42nd floor about an opportunity for more convenient coordination between the investment department and the accounting department that should improve the bottom line.

All you wanted was an office where your feet would not freeze, you wouldn't break out in a rash from the heat, or you wouldn't have to walk four floors when the elevator didn't work.

Now, though, the people on the 42nd floor are happy for the extra "bottom line." Your manager is happy because the top people accepted his or her carefully thought-out suggestion (which he got from you). You, too, are going to be happy because you are going to be remembered. So your feet are going to be warm for the first time this winter. In addition, just before the supervisor leaves the big people on the 42nd floor, he or she suggests that your salary increase be approved.

You may think this is an over-simplification, but it may be more closely related to an actual promotion or pay raise than you realize. Yesterday, the situation was such that you were ready to risk a job change, and today you are a star with the organization. It happened because you didn't "bail out" too soon but took creative action.

10

OWNERSHIP OR MANAGEMENT WHO "MAKE THE MONEY"

When we enter the job market, it does not take many coffee breaks before many of us learn there are many rungs on the management ladder. Usually the larger the company or organization, the more rungs on the ladder.

In my own career I took a good look at the ladder and decided I wanted to climb as high and as quickly as possible. The position became more important than the money.

Each step up the ladder resulted in a high degree of satisfaction. I was willing to pack up my family and move for very little increase in compensation because it was one more step up the ladder. Some companies make such moves financially rewarding, and others let you enjoy status more than compensation.

Take a close look at your company and see where the ownership is. If you are highly paid for your contribution to the organization, you might need to be happy with that and just enjoy the good life. Ultimately, however, having some ownership in the company will probably be best for your career.

In most corporations, there are many ways to increase your personal wealth while you climb the corporate ladder. Here are a few:

- 401-K RETIREMENT PLANS

- STOCK OPTIONS

- PROFIT SHARING

- DIVIDENDS FROM STOCK

- STOCK SPLITS

- MAJOR MEDICAL INSURANCE

- GROUP LIFE INSURANCE

- PAID VACATIONS

- (YOU ADD TO THE LIST.)

The smaller mid-sized companies might not have nearly as many rungs on the management ladder, but they may provide a much better opportunity for ownership.

For more than twenty years prior to moving to Rome, Georgia, the small city in which I now live, my family and I had lived in much larger cities—Jacksonville, Florida; Jackson and Chattanooga, Tennessee; Indianapolis, Indiana; and Lexington, Kentucky. Each of these moves provided a higher position and some increase in income.

We spent our first few days in Rome looking at houses with our realtor. I commented to the realtor about the many beautiful homes in a community of our size, about 40,000 in the city and about 40,000 more in the surrounding county. He said that the community has a number of small business owners and a few corporate executives. The small businesses include sole proprietors, partnerships, and closely-held corporations. These businesses provide great income for their individual owners. Many of these businesses have been in the same family for many years. These businesses have provided fine homes, shiny automobiles, boats, planes, second homes, good education for the children, and other such "finer things of life." Professional corporations—CPAs, attorneys, doctors, and dentists—have done equally as well. Most well-educated persons providing a personal service can expect to be compensated well for their service.

Be sure to keep in mind both possibilities—moving into business ownership and moving up the management ladder—as you try to make the most of your earning potential.

Part II.

IT'S WHAT'S INSIDE THAT COUNTS

11

Winners and Losers

The world loves a winner. Some say winning is not everything, and others believe winning is the only thing. Some will say winning is not that important, but what's important is how you play the game. Some say that a tie game is like kissing your sister or brother. Remember, though, that winners keep score. All other things being equal, *winning* is more fun than *losing*.

The 1996 Olympic Games, held in Atlanta, were historic. Never in history has the South pulled together and invited the world to be our guest. We have small towns in Georgia with 500 to 3,500 residents who saw their population grow to as many as 10,000 people the day the Olympic torch arrived in town. This occurrence was repeated not only in Georgia but all over the country.

Young people came from many countries all over the world. They spoke languages we did not understand, and they could not understand us. They all understood a smile, a hug, a handshake, and a taste of our Southern-cooked food, though. I will say that some of them didn't think grits and greens were too tasty, however.

One young woman said to me in broken English, "Mr. Tillman, you have very different accent. Do you have what we have heard many people call a Southern drawl? Do all people in your country have the wonderful drawl?"

By this time I was sure that if she did not win a gold medal in her event, she would not return home without a shoe box full of medals in public relationships. I assured her we also had other wonderful accents in cities like New York, Boston, Dallas, and New Orleans. I told her we had all been winners because of her visit and the visits of the people from around the world.

From the announcement, "Let the games begin," to the time

the last person finished his or her event, everyone knew that all Olympic participants were winners just by being at the Olympics. Not all who competed received the gold medal, of course. Each, though, had won many times in competition in his or her own country. Each came to Atlanta to compete with other world-class winners from all over the world. Those of us who watched, cheered, and pulled for our special person or team wished for them health and the opportunity to do their very best. We knew they were all winners.

Reading this book indicates that you are a winner. Take a look at the following list of winners and losers.

- A WINNER KNOWS THAT PEOPLE WILL BE KIND IF YOU GIVE THEM A CHANCE. A LOSER FEELS THAT PEOPLE WILL BE UNKIND IF YOU GIVE THEM THE CHANCE.

- A WINNER ISN'T NEARLY AS AFRAID OF LOSING AS A LOSER IS SECRETLY AFRAID OF WINNING.

- A WINNER WORKS HARDER THAN A LOSER AND HAS MORE TIME. A LOSER IS ALWAYS "TOO BUSY" TO DO WHAT IS NECESSARY.

- A WINNER TAKES A BIG PROBLEM AND SEPARATES IT INTO SMALLER PARTS SO IT CAN BE SOLVED MORE EASILY. A LOSER TAKES A LOT OF LITTLE PROBLEMS AND ROLLS THEM TOGETHER UNTIL THEY CANNOT BE SOLVED.

- A WINNER MAKES COMMITMENTS; A LOSER MAKES PROMISES.

- A WINNER SAYS, "I'M GOOD, BUT NOT AS GOOD AS I OUGHT TO BE." A LOSER SAYS, "I'M NOT AS BAD AS A LOT OF OTHER PEOPLE."

- A WINNER LISTENS. A LOSER JUST WAITS UNTIL IT'S HIS OR HER TURN TO SPEAK.

- A WINNER IS SENSITIVE TO THE SURROUNDING ATMOSPHERE. A LOSER IS SENSITIVE ONLY TO HIS OR HER OWN FEELINGS.

- A WINNER RESPECTS THOSE WHO ARE SUPERIOR AND TRIES TO LEARN FROM THEM. A LOSER RESENTS THOSE WHO ARE SUPERIOR AND TRIES TO FIND CHINKS IN THEIR ARMOR.

- A WINNER SAYS, "THERE OUGHT TO BE A BETTER WAY TO DO IT." A LOSER SAYS, "THAT'S THE WAY IT'S ALWAYS BEEN DONE."

- AS A WINNER, YOU MAY WANT TO ADD TO THIS LIST YOUR-SELF.

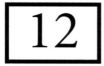

SUCCESS AND FAILURE

Some time ago I was speaking to a sales organization in Indianapolis, Indiana. The Hoosiers are great people and know just how to cut through the small talk.

I had just read Eddie Fisher's book about his life. As you probably know, in the '50s and '60s and even later on, Eddie Fisher had girls fainting with just about every note in every song he sang. Many mothers picked him as the ideal son-in-law.

So often, though, we may have outstanding success in our careers and failure in our personal lives. Most will tell you we need success in both.

The life Eddie Fisher lived was one of great success but also of great failure. In the speech, I mentioned his marriages to the beautiful and exciting Debbie Reynolds; to another great beauty and star, Elizabeth Taylor; then to another wonderful and talented beauty, Connie Stevens; then to another and another. About that time a man way in the back in a very large auditorium filled with many people yelled, "Hey, mister, he's doing better failing than we are succeeding!"

The man did make a good point. (On second thought, maybe I should have said, "Speak for yourself, buddy!") Still, I wish for you success in both your career and your personal life.

A surgeon friend of mine has a big practice fixing people's perceived physical imperfections. He builds some up, cuts some down, changes direction of some things, and in general does a right good job. The magazine and book racks are filled with literature about this kind of "fixing." Some people even feel this kind of "fixing" is imperative for their careers, good looks, and self-esteem.

I might even consider it myself if I were not afraid of needles and sharp knives. I never much wanted to bother the Lord's work if it could not be fixed with dieting. Unless there is a medical problem, the Lord did a fair enough job on most of us—better on some than others.

Most mothers know the importance of telling their daughters they are beautiful and their sons they are handsome. They temper that with caution that beauty is only skin deep and beauty is as beauty does.

In their early years, many young girls and boys are hit pretty hard by their peers with statements like "Big Butt Bertha" or "Four-eyed Charlie." Some of these scars are hard to correct with the best surgery. However, most teachers, parents, and good friends are always looking to add positive admiration and affirmation for the young men and women. It's good when we can bring these healthy affirmations to the workplace. They are a significant part of achieving true success.

13

A Society of Ph.D.s and Fourth-Grade Emotions

Someone has indicated that people have more formal education today than at any other time in our history. We have sons and daughters completing high school, college, and graduate school, while their parents and grandparents had little formal education. Unfortunately, it seems sometimes that many graduates did not grow with their emotions as much as they grew with their formal education.

It is important to be on the lookout for the big degree on the wall and the fourth-grade emotion behind the desk. You may have learned already about the importance of your supervisor's emotions, especially how they affect you.

You might take a good look, though, at yourself and see how fragile your own emotions are. You might need to take a good look in the mirror and say to yourself, "I am beautiful/handsome. I am God's creation. I am somebody. This is the day the Lord has made, and He made it for me."

Consider a few "do's" along the way:

- DO "HANG OUT" WITH POSITIVE PEOPLE.

- DO ASSOCIATE WITH THE "UP AND AT-EM."

- DO BUILD UP OTHERS.

- DO BUILD UP YOUR COMPANY OR ORGANIZATION.

- DO REMEMBER TO ASK YOUR SUPERVISOR, "HOW AM I DOING?"

Remember to try and make your business and career decisions with your mind, using all the education and training you have received, not your fourth-grade emotions. Also, remember that although people in high positions may have lots of education, experience, and training, they sometimes are in the fourth grade with their emotions. Some days you yourself may revert to those fourth-grade emotions. Watch yourself on those days, especially. Try to avoid making the big decisions then.

14

EDUCATION

Education—get all you can, and take all you can to the workplace. It will help you *get* the job. To *keep* the job requires hard work, interest in the organization, and concern for helping your company and other people—especially your immediate supervisor—achieve their goals and objectives.

Most industries have their own training programs, with courses related to their area of work. Take them. Your leader needs all the plusses he or she can have in your behalf when presenting your raise and promotion to the higher-ups.

15

Eat Right and Get Enough Exercise

Your parents probably told you, "Eat right and get enough sleep and exercise." Now you know they were right. If your supervisor is on the trim side, you might as well plan to take off about twenty pounds. It may help to bring your parents by the office to let the leadership know that your whole family is a "little stocky." Point out, too, that you over-compensate with good looks, enthusiasm, a strong work ethic, a big smile, and loyalty to the company.

So here is my recommended diet:

BREAKFAST

1/2 GRAPEFRUIT

3/4 CUP CORN FLAKES

1/2 CUP SKIM MILK

1 CUP COFFEE, BLACK

LUNCH

1 BAKED CHICKEN BREAST, SKIN REMOVED

LETTUCE AND TOMATO SALAD

2 TABLESPOONS LOW-FAT DRESSING

1/2 CUP GREEN BEANS

1 SLICE WHOLE WHEAT BREAD, NO BUTTER

2 CHOCOLATE CHIP COOKIES

FOUR P.M. SNACK

1 CUP HOT CHOCOLATE

REST OF THE BAG OF CHOCOLATE CHIP COOKIES

DINNER

SALAD, WITH THOUSAND ISLAND DRESSING

10-OUNCE STEAK

BAKED POTATO, WITH SOUR CREAM AND BUTTER

2 ROLLS, WITH BUTTER

CHOCOLATE CHEESECAKE WITH STRAWBERRY ICE CREAM ON
   THE SIDE

BEDTIME SNACK

ANOTHER PIECE OF CHEESECAKE (NO ICE CREAM)

We have spent most of this book so far with the "do's," but you already know that the foods you don't eat are as important as the ones you do eat. A good, balanced diet is important. This subject is not to be taken lightly. Maybe we could have lunch together sometime and talk about it.

Exercise is also very important to your success in business as well as in life. I love to walk each day. Lots of big and little problems have been solved with a good walk with a friend or co-worker.

I admire the jogger, even though the expression on the faces of joggers seems to indicate pain. I'm hoping I'll make enough money sometime that I will be able to hire someone to do my jogging. (I don't take jogging lightly either, though. My son, who was quite successful in track and cross-country in college and is now a successful businessman, gets bent all out of shape if he does not get to jog or ride his fancy bike several miles each week.)

Here's a way to blend getting your exercise with getting your raise or promotion. Walk or jog with your supervisor. If you can pull that off, you become the listener and the support person as your supervisor deals with all the tension and frustration of the day. Some people do not like to talk business during a walk, but, believe me, the movers and shakers do just that.

16

DRESS APPROPRIATELY

I shall never forget a young man who came to our office. He had an excellent formal education. He also had an excellent command of the English language. Any English teacher would have been proud of him. He put the "-ing" on all the right words and didn't use any dangling participles. I would not have known this myself, but one of my associates picked up on his great verbal skill.

This very gifted young man met the paper requirements of the position. Then he asked me what I thought of his long hair and cross-shaped earrings. I assured him his hair looked well-combed and neat. The young man's earrings were long enough and shiny enough to be very noticeable. Then he told me how much his girl friend loved his long hair. Too, the earrings were a special gift from her and thus had a special meaning.

The young man asked me some difficult questions. He asked whether it would be necessary for him to get his hair cut for the executive sales position we were offering.

My own training has taught me to answer a question with a question. I asked him what percent of the people in our town might have some definite feelings about doing business with him and whether his long hair and earrings would make a difference.

He replied, "Oh, I know the people in this town, and probably 75% would not buy from me."

"Our business is tough," I suggested, "even when we project the young executive image. By your own admission, only 25% of the people will be willing to do business with you. If the entire 25% buys from you, then you have an opportunity to be very successful in our business."

The last time I heard from him, he was a professional musician, and his concerts were sell-outs. We gave him an opportunity to decide for himself and to stick with his conviction. He knew his market.

Dress is important. Some supervisors break out in a rash when they see unshined shoes or runs in stockings. One of my associates said our company president looks at your shoes before he looks you in the eye. I do know that his father was in the military and that the president carries a shoebrush and shoe polish when traveling.

A certain dress pattern is considered proper in each industry. Find what style of dress is appropriate for your industry. If you do not play by the rules of your industry, you will find it tough to climb the success ladder very fast. There are always exceptions, of course, but be prepared to make that exception something that makes the top floor very happy.

Appropriate dress also takes in your attitude. Successful folks will tell you that attitude determines altitude. So a "check up from the neck up" is also an important part of the kind of appearance that is appropriate and that will get you up the organization toward promotions and pay raises.

17

Toward a Positive Attitude

Nothing will assure you of success any more than a positive attitude. Here are five giant steps that will put you out front.

I. Take a new look at your life. Your attitude today about yourself, your life, your profession, and your future may be largely a composite of the attitudes of others—parents, teachers, friends, and peers. You may need to change your attitude. You may need to take a new look at your life, through your own eyes, and learn to think positively about your potentials and possibilities.

II. You must like yourself. You will never like someone else more than you really like yourself. Also, other people tend to take the same attitude toward you that you take toward yourself.

III. You must develop a genuine concern for and interest in other people. Successful people are always "other-oriented."

IV. Begin every day in a spirit of gratitude and with a sense of genuine expectancy that today will be the greatest day of your life.

V. Keep your dreams. When you quit dreaming, you quit looking forward to life.

18

YOU THINK *YOU* HAVE A PROBLEM

You may feel you have a franchise on all the problems. You may feel if anything can go wrong at work, it went wrong for you this day, this week, or this month. You may feel everything that can go wrong at home has gone wrong. The stove broke, the dishwasher went from automatic to overflow, and the car had two flat tires.

Well, if you feel you have a franchise on most of the problems of the world, just think of your minister, preacher, pastor, or bishop, who has been so busy preparing a message for Sunday, visiting the sick, and conducting funerals and weddings. He's just been too busy to proof the church bulletin for Sunday. The following are a few actual excerpts from church bulletins that will help you see the problem and I hope give you a chuckle.

- THIS AFTERNOON THERE WILL BE A BAPTISMAL IN THE SOUTH AND NORTH ENDS OF THE CHURCH. CHILDREN WILL BE BAPTIZED AT BOTH ENDS.

- TUESDAY AT 4 P.M. THERE WILL BE AN ICE CREAM SOCIAL. ALL LADIES GIVING MILK PLEASE COME EARLY.

- WEDNESDAY, THE LADIES' LITERARY SOCIETY WILL MEET. MRS. JOHNSON WILL SING, "PUT ME IN MY LITTLE BED ACCOMPANIED BY THE PASTOR."

- THIS BEING EASTER SUNDAY, WE WILL ASK MRS. JONES TO COME FORWARD AND LAY AN EGG ON THE ALTAR.

- THE SERVICE WILL CLOSE WITH "LITTLE DROPS OF WATER." ONE OF THE LADIES WILL START QUIETLY, AND THE REST OF THE CONGREGATION WILL JOIN IN.

- THIS MORNING A SPECIAL COLLECTION WILL BE TAKEN TO DEFRAY THE EXPENSES ON THE NEW CARPET. ALL WISHING TO DO SOMETHING ON THE CARPET, PLEASE COME FORWARD AND GET A PIECE OF PAPER.

- THE LADIES OF THE CHURCH HAVE CAST OFF CLOTHING OF EVERY KIND, AND THEY MAY BE SEEN IN THE CHURCH BASEMENT ON FRIDAY AFTERNOON.

- THIS EVENING AT 7 P.M. THERE WILL BE A HYMN SING IN THE PARK ACROSS FROM THE CHURCH. BRING A BLANKET AND COME PREPARED TO SIN.

- IF YOU HAVE CHILDREN AND DO NOT KNOW IT, THE NURSERY IS ON THE SECOND FLOOR.

19

THE BEST THINGS IN LIFE ARE PRICELESS

Every effort is being made in this book to give you ideas that will help you have the good life financially. Remember, though, the best things in life are priceless. They include:

- THE VALUE OF TIME

- THE SUCCESS OF PERSEVERANCE

- THE PLEASURE OF WORKING

- THE DIGNITY OF SIMPLICITY

- THE WORTH OF CHARACTER

- THE INFLUENCE OF EXAMPLE

- THE OBLIGATION OF DUTY

- THE WISDOM OF ECONOMY

- THE VIRTUE OF PATIENCE

- THE IMPROVEMENT OF TALENT

- THE JOY OF ORGANIZATION

- THE FULFILLMENT OF A JOB WELL DONE

- THE SATISFACTION OF SERVICE

- THE POWER OF KNOWLEDGE

20

THE MIXON ATTITUDE

A few days ago I was talking with Dr. Frank Arnold, my wife Carolyn's first cousin. After retirement he returned to his grandfather's farm to live. He has a lovely home, but he left the old house standing, since it is the place of his boyhood memories. He has done all the good things that a successful life brings. Now he is happy to get on his tractor, hook up the trailer, and take his children, grandchildren, and cousins for a slow ride through the woods to check to see how high the water is in the creek.

A man named Mixon lived on the farm with Dr. Arnold's grandmother and grandfather. He lived in their house, and the grandchildren had the run of the house. However, since Mixon was not a family member, the privacy of his room was respected. The grandchildren could not run in and out of Mixon's room unless invited to do so. Mixon was provided a place to live, plenty to eat, and $2.75 per week. He had to pay for his own haircut from the wages. Ordinary haircuts were 10 cents, but if someone had been to town to receive additional training and thus knew the style of the day the cut was 25 cents.

This was in the mid to late 30s. The depression had ended in the North, but the news had not reached the South yet.

Soon President Roosevelt announced that the United States would enter World War II. Our nation called young men from the farms, factories, and offices to fight for the freedom of our land and for people in other parts of the world. Many women would join this fight, and men and women of all ages would support this effort on the home front.

Many young men and women left their homes for the first time. Mixon received word and knew it was his last day to plow for a long time if ever again. Dr. Arnold remembered that Mixon had taught him to plow. Plowing a mule was a way of earning a living for Mixon but just plain fun for a town boy visiting his grandparents for the summer.

Dr. Arnold remembers that Mixon took great pride in plowing a straight row and making the field as perfect as possible for corn, cotton, or beans to grow. But most of all Dr. Arnold remembered Mixon's positive attitude toward his work and his patience in teaching a young boy a skill he had learned over many hours of looking at the south end of a northbound mule.

About 200 miles east, as a young boy I had learned the same skills on a southeast Georgia farm. Since I lived on the farm with my family year round and did not return to the city in the fall, I sometimes do not remember those tough days with the same feelings that Dr. Arnold does.

After Mixon went to the army, he wrote home with all the excitement of a young boy at Boy Scout camp. Mixon told about his nice new clothes, free room and board, and free haircuts, plus the $21.00 per month he received in wages. Too, he had met young men from New York, New Jersey, Pittsburgh, Boston, California, and other places. They all talked a little funny to Mixon. They asked him where he was from and what he did. Sometimes they would ask him questions just to get him to talk.

Mixon was used to eating rice, grits, corn on the cob, green beans, tomatoes, ham, beef, and fried chicken. Any of those dishes plus any new ones were just fine with him. Some of his new friends wanted pizza or lasagna. Mixon didn't know about these dishes, but he felt that they must be good since his new friends appeared to be mighty smart about lots of things.

Most of us would say Mixon had a great attitude. Mixon took a situation and made the best of it. Some might say Mixon was not too smart. Others may say he just did not know any better, but most of us would agree that Mixon gave it his best.

Mixon had what you are going to need if you don't already have it: a positive attitude. The following "Attitude Commandments" will serve you well:

- ATTITUDE, NOT APTITUDE, GOVERNS ALTITUDE.

- THE PURPOSE OF EXISTENCE IS NOT TO MAKE A LIVING BUT TO MAKE A LIFE.

- CHARACTER IS NOT INHERENT. EACH INDIVIDUAL BUILDS HIS OR HER OWN.

- THE ULTIMATE COST OF SOMETHING IS THE AMOUNT OF YOUR LIFE THAT YOU WILL EXCHANGE FOR IT.

- YOUTH IS NOT A TIME OF LIFE BUT A STATE OF MIND. WRINKLES TEST THE SKIN BUT NEVER TOUCH THE SOUL.

- PEOPLE WHO HAVE NOT SET A WORTHWHILE PURPOSE FOR THEIR LIVES ARE EASY PREY FOR ANXIETY.

- THE WORST BANKRUPTCY IS LOSING YOUR ENTHUSIASM.

- NOBODY CAN MAKE YOU FEEL INFERIOR WITHOUT YOUR CONSENT.

21

MAINTAIN ENTHUSIASM AND USE A CHECKLIST

Yesterday I zipped across two states at 200 miles per hour. After taking off, I did not see the ground again until just a few minutes before landing. I trusted the instruments, and the steady hum of the engine took me exactly where I wanted to go.

As all pilots do, I used a checklist before I took off. That's what you need to do in life, too. Use a checklist before you take off. Check your cruise list en route, and be sure you check your landing list twice.

Use the following checklist to see how you are doing with your enthusiasm:

- CONSTANTLY IMPROVE YOURSELF. FOR EXAMPLE, TAKE EDUCATIONAL COURSES, READ ON YOUR OWN, IMPROVE YOUR MEMORY, OR IMPROVE YOUR SPEAKING VOICE. KNOWING THAT IN SOME WAY YOU WILL BE BETTER A MONTH FROM NOW THAN YOU ARE TODAY PROVIDES A POSITIVE FORCE.

- ACT ENTHUSIASTIC. WALK AS IF YOU ARE EXCITED ABOUT GETTING TO YOUR DESTINATION. MAINTAIN GOOD POSTURE. READ MOTIVATIONAL STORIES.

- SPEAK ONLY IN POSITIVE TERMS. SHUN PESSIMISTIC ATTITUDES. ALWAYS LOOK FOR THE POSITIVE WAY OF LOOKING AT THINGS, BECAUSE IT'S THERE.

- SPEND TIME DOING THINGS THAT ARE HIGHLY INTERESTING TO YOU, AND YOU WILL BECOME A MORE INTERESTING PERSON. GET INVOLVED IN WORTHWHILE CAUSES.

- ACCOMPLISH SOMETHING. DO THE THINGS YOU HAVE BEEN PUTTING OFF. GET TO WORK EARLY SOMETIMES, AND STAY LATE. ACCOMPLISHMENTS, WHATEVER THEY MAY BE, WILL CREATE ENTHUSIASM.

- LEARN MORE ABOUT YOUR JOB. KNOWLEDGE TENDS TO MAKE FOR INTEREST, AND INTEREST MAKES FOR ENTHUSIASM.

- SET A GOAL.

- CHALLENGE YOURSELF.

- MAKE YOURSELF A WINNER.

Read the following checklist when you feel you need help in staying motivated:

- REALLY LISTEN TO EVERYONE YOU MEET. IF YOU ARE INTERESTED IN PEOPLE, LIFE WILL ALWAYS HAVE MEANING AND DIRECTION.

- ACT ENTHUSIASTIC. IT MAKES YOU FEEL ENTHUSIASTIC AND HAS THE SAME EFFECT ON PEOPLE AROUND YOU.

- KEEP YOUR JOB CHALLENGING. ALWAYS REACH FOR SOMETHING.

- KEEP BUSY. WHEN YOU ARE ACTIVE, IT IS IMPOSSIBLE TO BE UNMOTIVATED.

- READ. READING WILL BUILD YOUR STORE OF KNOWLEDGE, PRESENT YOU WITH NEW IDEAS, AND PROVIDE PLENTY OF STIMULATION.

- DO IT YOURSELF. CREATING SOMETHING IS A GOOD WAY TO STAVE OFF BOREDOM AND PROVIDE A SENSE OF ACHIEVEMENT.

22

IT IS IMPORTANT TO LIKE TO WORK

Most people like to work. That is not to say they like their work, but most like and want the gratification that comes from work. Since we spend much of our life working, it is important to do worthwhile work. Try to spend your time doing something you really enjoy.

It's also important to understand that some jobs are like some people. All aspects of the job will not be perfect.

Most companies and organizations have excellent test instruments to give you an idea of your aptitude. If you are in management, you will want to use all available resources to select the right person for the job. However, I believe most of us can be very happy doing many different jobs if we are given the opportunity for training.

23

Is Your Job Title Important to You?

Most of us want an increase in pay to give us a better standard of living. In addition, we want a promotion as a way of recognizing our efforts. Most of us want to be "somebody." Most parents will tell their children at an early age to remember who they are. They will also remind their children that they are important.

Many years ago when I was in college, I worked for Grant's Department Store during the Christmas holidays. Grant's did a great job of making young men and women feel important. The lady who hired the college and high school students for the Christmas jobs was a master at getting the most out of people. Each of us had a name tag and a title.

In those days, most of us had just moved to town from the farm. I can still remember going back to our little country church one Sunday and hearing a grandmother brag on her grandson Hershel who was assistant manager of Grant's Department Store in Jacksonville, Florida. I'm sure my cousin Hershel had told his grandmother what his position was but had just mumbled over some of the minor details.

Cousin Hershel's real position was the assistant manager of the candy department of Grant's Department Store on the second shift. That title was fine on Saturday at 8 p.m. when he was standing behind the counter selling a pound of candy. We never told his grandmother the correct title, and one day Hershel was in fact assistant manager.

Just remember one thing more about most titles. They are important to us, our co-workers, and our grandmothers. The rest of the world does not really care.

24

Do You Have a Sense of Urgency or a Curse of Procrastination?

Have a sense of urgency about your work, a "do-it-now" attitude. If there is some item on your list that you are putting off until another time, do it now, do it first, and get it behind you. If you don't, the rest of your day you will be thinking about it. It will be the "monkey on your back" until the job is complete.

Procrastination affects us all. A friend has come up with an idea that works right well for him. He says, "I'll do it tomorrow or the next day. I'm not sure that needs to be done this week. I don't believe I'll do it at all." That attitude may be OK if it does not affect your ultimate goal or the team effort. That attitude will most definitely affect adversely your raise or promotion, though.

25

Blue Ribbons From Doing What Is Expected

During my early years, my family lived ten miles from town. One set of grandparents lived one mile south of us, and the other grandparents lived three miles north of us. My mother would sometimes need to borrow a cup of sugar, coffee, or flour from a neighbor or relative. She would tell my twin brother Ed and me to go and borrow a cup of sugar and come right back. Ed and I would race each other all the way to our grandparents' house, get what our mother wanted, and race back home.

Not long ago Ed and I visited our high school track coach, Raymond Douglas. He mentioned that we were two of the best track athletes he had ever coached. Hearing that was a little embarrassing because we never viewed ourselves as athletes.

Our coach asked, "By the way, how did you boys learn to run so well?"

I replied, "By going for a cup of sugar."

I drove home that day a little taller. When I returned home, I found the shoe box of blue ribbons from those track events. Isn't it sometimes amazing how doing what is expected of you pays off in unexpected ways?

26

Ten Commandments of Success

1. WORK HARD.

2. STUDY HARD.

3. TAKE INITIATIVE.

4. LOVE YOUR WORK.

5. BE EXACT.

6. HAVE A SPIRIT OF CONQUEST.

7. CULTIVATE YOUR PERSONALITY.

8. HELP AND SHARE WITH OTHERS.

9. BE DEMOCRATIC.

10. ALWAYS DO YOUR BEST.

27

DON'T SLAP THE HAND THAT FEEDS YOU

Some employees seldom say a positive word about their company or organization. If you do not feel positively about your job and you dislike the company, your supervisor, and the products the company makes, then quit. Resign!

"Oh!" you say, "I can't quit, I need the money." Then keep quiet until you can find another job. The person working next to you may be very happy and does not need to hear negative talk.

Someone said misery loves company, so if you are in a department with a person who is always saying negative things about the company, don't listen to that person. Stay out of the person's way as much as possible. Many of us are like Forrest Gump: we feel life is pretty wonderful if the negative folks will not bother us. Also, if you feel you have a special talent to train, educate, or supervise a negative person so that the person becomes a positive, productive employee, the pay raise or promotion is waiting for you.

Sometimes at work I enjoy playing games with fellow employees. I'll start naming all the wonderful features of our jobs:

- DAYS OFF—CHRISTMAS DAY, THANKSGIVING WEEKEND, 4TH OF JULY, MEMORIAL DAY, EASTER WEEKEND, SICK DAYS WITH PAY, TIME OFF TO HAVE A BABY, PAID VACATION

- THIRTY-MINUTE LUNCH

- HOSPITAL INSURANCE

- INSURANCE FOR VISITS TO THE DOCTOR

- LIFE INSURANCE

- RETIREMENT PLAN

- COMPANY CONTRIBUTION TO SOCIAL SECURITY

- COMPANY-SPONSORED SAVINGS, 401(K) PLAN

- YMCA MEMBERSHIP

The list goes on, plus every two weeks we get a pay check, at Christmas a bonus, and then a raise at year end or on the anniversary of our employment. You could add to this list from your company or organization, I'm sure, items like continuing education, association memberships, and incentive or convention trips.

Many years ago when I was a young man on a small southern farm, I had very few of the items I just listed. Oh, yes, we had a fine quality of life, plenty to eat, friends, family that loved us, and a safe place to live. Since the rural way of life is not the way most of us live anymore, however, we need to take a good look at what the modern company or organization has provided us. Being grateful for our organization is a good way to get in line for a raise or promotion.

28

WORDS TO THE WISE

- NEVER LOSE YOUR CAPACITY FOR ENTHUSIASM.

- NEVER LOSE YOUR CAPACITY FOR INDIGNATION.

- IF YOU CAN'T BE GENEROUS WHEN IT'S HARD, YOU WON'T BE GENEROUS WHEN IT'S EASY.

- THE GREATEST CONFIDENCE-BUILDER IS THE ABILITY TO DO SOMETHING—ALMOST ANYTHING—WELL.

- THE WAY TO BE TRULY USEFUL IS TO DISCOVER THE BEST THAT OTHER PEOPLE'S BRAINS HAVE TO OFFER, USE THIS TO SUPPLEMENT YOUR OWN, AND GIVE CREDIT TO THEM WHEN THEY HAVE HELPED.

- THE GREATEST TRAGEDIES IN THE WORLD AND IN OUR PERSONAL LIVES STEM FROM MISUNDERSTANDINGS. TO AVOID THEM, LEARN TO COMMUNICATE WELL.

- DON'T JUST LET THINGS HAPPEN. IF YOU SEEK SUCCESS, YOU HAVE TO MAKE THEM HAPPEN.

29

TRUSTWORTHINESS

Are you trustworthy? Are you in a business or profession that is trustworthy? Does the general public feel you are trustworthy? Does the general public feel your business or profession is trustworthy? These are tough questions.

How we see ourselves and how others see us are sometimes miles apart. Surveys are interesting, even in the political world. If a survey reveals that a political candidate has a sizable lead in the polls, that political candidate accepts, praises, and quotes the survey data. However, the candidate who is several points behind in the polls takes the results with a grain of salt, at least when the candidate is talking with the press.

What kind of rating does the general public really give your business or profession? I recently saw a survey, which I'm going to share with you, about how the public perceives the trustworthiness of various professions.

I had some doubts about the survey and decided to conduct my own survey. I asked my seminar participants to pick the top three professions or businesses as to how trustworthy they are and then to name the bottom three. We then compared the results to the national survey. I was surprised how close our survey was to the national survey. Here's what the national survey revealed about the percent of the survey respondents who considered these professions trustworthy[1]:

---

[1] Source: Gallup poll of 1,229 US adults conducted Oct. 19-22, 1996. The results have a margin of sampling error of plus or minus .3 percentage points.

DRUGGIST •• 66%

CLERGY •• 56%

MEDICAL DOCTORS •••••••••••••••••••••••••••••••••••• 54%

DENTIST ••• 54%

ENGINEERS •••••••••••••••••••••••••••••••••••••• 53%

COLLEGE TEACHERS ••••••••••••••••••••••••••••• 52%

POLICEMEN •••••••••••••••••••••••••••••• 41%

BANKERS •••••••••••••••••••••• 27%

PUBLIC OPINION POLLSTERS ••••••••••• 25%

TV REPORTERS •••••••••••••• 21%

STOCKBROKERS ••••••••••• 16%

LAWYERS •••••••••••••• 15%

INSURANCE SALESMEN ••••• 11%

CONGRESSMAN/WOMAN •• 10%

CAR SALESPERSONS •• 5%

It is interesting that the druggist received the highest rating as to honesty and ethical standards. It is also interesting that the automobile salesman came out on the bottom. The Congress of the United States came out second from the bottom, and my own profession came out third from the bottom. What does this survey tell you about how people perceive your profession? What can you do about it?

Here is some more information to help you answer those questions. Out of 62,000 licensed insurance people in Georgia, only two or three people each month have their insurance license revoked, denied, or suspended. Is that a large number out of the total? The general public was asked, *Has an insurance person ever mistreated you?* Most said, *No.* Most thought their insurance person was honest and was a respected person in the community.

What about your representative in Congress? Do you like him or her? Most said, *Yes.* Have you ever been mistreated by your representative? Most said, *No.*

What about used car salespeople? When we looked more closely into this matter, we narrowed the field down to independent auto dealers. They are independent business people who belong to their dealer association. They have a code of ethics that calls them to be fair in their dealings with their customers. There are about seven thousand independent dealers in Florida and about the same number in Georgia. The other states seem to have about the same number as Georgia and Florida in proportion to the total population of the state.

Our survey asked the question: *Have you been mistreated by an Independent Automobile Dealer in your town or community?* Very few indicated they had been mistreated. We decided to ask one more question. *Would you feel more comfortable buying a used automobile from a local member of the Independent Automobile Dealer Association or someone from the general public?*

How would you feel? Most voted for the dealer. It is interesting that most trusted the independent businessperson more than they trusted the general public.

When we looked at the bottom line, the three businesses or professions that were ranked at the bottom of the national survey all received good marks when people were asked about their own insurance person, congressional representative, or auto salesperson.

Take a look at your own business or profession. Is your business or profession considered trustworthy? Whether it is or it isn't might not be as important as the perception people have. If your profession is trustworthy but is not perceived as being trustworthy, your work is still cut out for you. You must operate from a strong code of ethics in order to overcome the public's perception that you are not trustworthy.

For example, the Independent Automobile Dealer Association is making great advances in improving the public image of car dealers. Florida auto dealers have spent nearly a million dollars in the past few years to provide a home for battered women and children. Too, they are policing their industry for dealers who do not project a proper image or provide honest service. It may take a long time to change their public image, but they are making a special effort.

Look at your own business or profession and see what is being done or what should be done to maintain a strong ethical, trustworthy, public image. What did the druggist do to be ranked number one in honesty and ethical standards? Find out and do it.

Most businesses and professions are offering some continuing education in ethics. Most insurance people in Georgia are required to have ten to twenty hours each year of continuing education. Three of those hours must be in ethics. I have conducted the seminars for our company, the Georgia Life Underwriters Association, the Atlanta Life Underwriters Association, the Insurance Women of Georgia, and several other groups.

The fact is, ethics is good business. In most of our seminars, before we present any of the organized study material, we ask for a definition of ethics. Some will say ethics comes from the Greek word *ethos*, meaning custom or habitual mode of conduct. Some will say, ethics is "doing what is right." Others will quote the Golden Rule, and the list goes on and on. One woman in a seminar said, "Just do what your mama said do." That sounds like a good definition.

Did your mama ever tell you to get rich? Did she tell you to seek power? Did she tell you to bully others? Usually it's *no* to all these questions. What did she want for you? Most said she wanted them to be healthy, happy, get an education, be safe, be honest, be truthful, and do their best. She also wanted them to remember the good things they learned at home and school. She wanted them to be successful at whatever they chose as a profession or business so they could have a life as good as or better than hers.

In thinking about how to get a raise or promotion without asking, "Do what your Mama told you to do" should be high on your list. If you do what is right and ethical in our free enterprise system and the product you sell or service is needed within our society, you will be successful. Raises and promotions will be a part of this success.

Part III.

GETTING OUTSIDE—AND INSIDE—HELP

30

THE INSIDE CROWD AND
THE OUTSIDE CROWD

In most companies and organizations there are two groups, though many will not admit that these two groups exist. All in each group are treated fairly. All get the same breaks, the same opportunity for advancement in pay, responsibility, and position. Sometimes there is a very fine line between the two groups. It may be hard to find, but it's still there.

I've seen these two groups in churches, civic clubs, and other organizations. We might call the two groups the "in" group and the "out" group. Some might call the "ins" apple polishers or other names, but the "ins" call it good business.

I've been in both groups. I know it is more fun to be with the "in" crowd.

Usually the "ins" get up early, go to bed late, and work like crazy to get everything done that needs to be done. For the "in" group, it's fun to go to work. They know the possibility of a raise or promotion is there, but they don't say much about it.

The "ins" usually have the power, position, and perks. This is just as true at the entry-level position as it is on the 42nd floor. The "outs" look for sundown and payday and don't have very much fun or satisfaction from their work. I hope you're one of the "ins."

31

PERSONAL POWER AND POSITION POWER

It has been said that there are two kinds of power—personal power and position power. All of us have some of both. In the workplace, position power is something we seek. If there are three people in the candy department, and you are the manager of the candy department on the second shift, you have position power. It might not be important to the rest of the world, but it is important to you.

In our country, we look at the position of the President of the United States as the most powerful position. We spend much time and money to elect to that position the very best person. When the last vote is counted, 49% think the other 51% "messed up"! However, when the decision is made, we do whatever is necessary to protect that position. That position has the power (with the approval of our Congress) to commit our people and resources to defending our people against any outside aggression. History has revealed that persons with that power feel the awesome responsibility.

What about personal power? We gain personal power through our relationships with other people. If a person has only position power, when the position is gone there is not much left. Personal power is usually gained by service to other people.

Recently, a person who was responsible for one of the major political parties called and ask whether I would meet with their group and give consideration to running for an important position in our state. After the meeting and careful consideration, I expressed my appreciation and indicated the timing was not good for me. Maybe at this time I just did not have the "fire in my gut" for the race. At least that is what was indicated as a need to win. They boosted my ego by reviewing my state and community service and indicated they felt I could win.

The one thing I remember about the interview was an indictment against many who offer themselves for political office. The question to the new candidate by the news media is, "Why do you want this high office in your local, state, or national government?" The answer often is, "I want to serve the people. I want to be of service to my community, my state, and my country." That sounds so good it will nearly bring tears to the eyes of loyal, dedicated Americans.

The shocker is when the community leaders check the records of the candidate and find very little if any community service. How can you expect a person who has given very little community service to commit to full service to others?

Maybe a better answer by the candidate would be, "I want a position of power." The candidate probably would not get elected, but a history book would record an honest answer.

Recently, I have been watching a television program called "Biography." The program for an entire week told about powerful people. Most had been very important to the growth, success, and protection of our country.

One of those powerful and important people was Winston Churchill, the Prime Minister of Great Britain during World War II. His great strength was in encouraging his people during some of their darkest hours. Others profiled by the program led our own nation through some of the dark hours. All provided great examples of how a person who will not abuse position power can be used to save a nation.

What does it profit for people to gain the whole world and lose their own soul? I saw another mind-provoking quote the other day that relates to building and keeping wealth. It said, "You never see a U-Haul trailer being towed behind a hearse." That is a little harsh, but we all understand it.

During the difficult days of the stock market crash of 1929, men and women alike ended their lives because they did not keep them in proper perspective. To maintain a proper perspective on wealth,

I encourage you to get active in your church, community, government, and family.

How will you handle a crushing blow to your career? Sometimes it is hard for the downsizers of the world to understand the effect their actions have on individuals. Sometimes to save the company or organization, jobs must be cut, though. There is a good chance in your career that you will be terminated, fired, reassigned, downsized, transferred, or just laid off. At that time you are not thinking pay raise or promotion; you are thinking, "No paycheck this Friday."

Your confidence may be shattered when you lose your job, no matter the reason. I encourage you to maintain confidence in your ability. You may not have the same title or position after such a change, but you must remember you are the same person. You are still important to the people who really count, and you will do whatever is necessary to do the best you can for your family.

Many books have been written to help in this area, and lots of professional help is available. Too, just remember: You have a good name, you are willing to work, and you will make a comeback. Many times people are stronger than ever after such an experience. I was there once, and it is no fun. A little "nest egg" will give you that extra financial confidence you need.

Remember, your true friends don't really care whether you drive a pickup or a limousine, use regular or high-test, eat steak or hamburger, play golf or kick the can. Your true friends care about the well-being of you and your family.

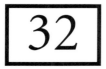

SERVICE TO OTHERS

The teacher said to her third-grade class, "We were put here on this earth to serve others." The little third-grade girl said, "Teacher, why were the others put here?"

We should not do service work to advance our own career, but almost all who have gained wealth and positions of leadership feel much of that gain came from service to others. We talked earlier about service to your community, church, industry association, alumni association, and political party. Since you will be able to achieve much more with and through others, you might consider becoming active in such groups.

Many young parents have little time for service activities outside the home. However, there are many service opportunities that will keep the family together and provide excellent opportunity for service. They include your church, Sunday School class, PTA, PTO, Junior Service League, and many fine civic clubs such as Kiwanis, Lions, Rotary, and Optimist. Toastmasters International will improve your speaking skills and prepare you for that special presentation that could boost your career.

Your own industry has an association, with local, state, and national chapters. They offer educational courses and opportunities to travel to meetings. Participation keeps you current in your business or profession.

Most companies take a close look at what you do in your industry. The contacts you make plus your personal growth will be great for your career. Each time your picture appears in the paper or your name is mentioned on the radio or television, your company may be mentioned. This shows the folks on the 42nd floor that you have qualities of leadership. Don't neglect service to others.

33

NETWORKING

Networking seems to be the buzzword going around today. It is important to know as many people as you can in your own company and industry.

You will also find that membership in your local, state, and national organizations provides significant benefits, for several reasons. These organizations provide great educational opportunities, offer excellent resources for information you might need, and keep you abreast of what's new in your industry, including ideas you may be able to apply in your company. In addition, if you ever need to change your place of employment, a couple of phone calls to key people may keep you from missing a paycheck.

34

HOW THE ORGANIZATION WORKS

Almost everyone answers to someone. As we enter the job market, it seems everyone has it better than we do. You might feel, "One day I'll be manager or supervisor of the department. Or, I'll be vice president or president, and I will not have to spend my time answering to someone." That situation will never be in today's business or professional world.

Of course, you might form your own business. However, most people who own their own businesses will quickly tell you that they answer to their clients or customers. In the field of medicine, the doctors will quickly tell you they answer to their patients. Many doctors have told me how aware they are of their patients' time. The old idea of just accepting long waits in a doctor's office is vanishing. Patients will get up and leave if there is a long wait each time they visit their doctor; they will find a doctor who is more considerate of their time. So one of the most respected professions still answers to the consumer.

In the modern corporation, the reporting looks something like this: the employee to a supervisor, the supervisor to a department manager, the manager to the assistant vice president, the vice president to the president, the president to the chairman of the board, the board chairman to the board, and the board to the stockholders.

Recently, I've had the opportunity to visit with some company presidents and find that their evaluation by the board is as comprehensive as that of the entry-level employee in the organization. So whatever your position, the old saying applies: "When the spotlight hits you, you'd better be dancing."

To make this point in a little more emphatic manner, consider the "Law of the Jungle."

Each morning when the antelope wakes up, it knows it must run faster than the fastest lion in order to survive that day. Every morning when the lion wakes up, it knows it must outrun the slowest antelope or it will starve to death. So, when the sun comes up, it does not matter whether you are a lion or an antelope, you had better be running.

35

USE "THE POWER OF THE PEN"

Every year we receive many graduation and wedding announcements. Like most, we try to send a nice gift. We are grateful that young people consider us a friend of their family and care enough to let us know of their achievements or, in case of a wedding, to share in the family happiness.

We don't keep a written record of the responses, but it seems we recall who did or did not say "thank you." One young lady either wrote her thank-you notes on her honeymoon or mailed them then. They were postmarked from the honeymoon destination. I'm not sure how Ann or Abby say to respond, but I do know when the first happy announcement for baby number one is received we don't break down the gift store door unless those high school, college, and wedding gifts were acknowledged.

I don't know who is giving the training to the young people in our town, but most of the young people are very good to acknowledge gifts received. Probably their parents get the credit for teaching their young folks what I call "the power of the pen."

A few weeks ago I was invited to the be the guest speaker at Coosa High School's Cooperative Business Education Employer-Employee Luncheon. This organization sponsors young people to work and go to school. Several awards were given to both students and employers. Officers in the club conducted the meeting, including introducing the employees, the guests, and the guest speaker. The entire program was training at its best. If the program had ended there, we would have all had a good day.

A few days later I received personal letters from each of the students. Some said the speaker was excellent, some pointed out specific parts of the presentation, and others expressed gratitude for the school, the employers, and the speaker for making the luncheon a special occasion for them. I don't know whose idea it was to write such nice personal letters, but my hat is off to the students, their employers, and Ms. Kay Shahan, the Cooperative Business Education Coordinator.

All of these experiences reinforce the idea of the "power of the pen." Some may think of the "power of the pen" as just "apple polishing" or "buttering up the boss." Consider the following and if either the boss or a co-worker deem the action as either one of these, then it is their problem and not yours.

- BE SINCERE.

- SELECT A SPECIAL TIME, LIKE THANKSGIVING OR YOUR ANNIVERSARY WITH THE COMPANY OR ORGANIZATION.

- WRITE THE PRESIDENT A LETTER AND TELL HOW GRATEFUL YOU ARE FOR YOUR POSITION WITH THE COMPANY AND FOR THE MANY WAYS THE COMPANY HAS HELPED YOU AND YOUR FAMILY. TELL OF YOUR BELIEF IN THE COMPANY'S PRODUCTS

AND SERVICES. EXPRESS GRATITUDE FOR BEING PART OF THE COMPANY. MENTION THE PEOPLE WHO HAVE HELPED YOU BECOME SUCCESSFUL.

- IF YOU TYPE THE LETTER, SEND YOUR SUPERVISOR AND OTHERS MENTIONED IN THE LETTER A BLIND COPY WITH A HANDWRITTEN NOTE TO THEM.

- TRY TO DO THIS WITHOUT EXPECTATION OF A RAISE OR PRO-MOTION.

Using the power of the pen to show appreciation for the people who help you, for the company management who have given you an opportunity, and for people who have provided you leadership and guidance can lead you to new heights in your career. *Do it!*

36

GIVING A SPEECH

Someone seems always to be doing research on the greatest fear. Flying in an airplane, getting too close to snakes, dealing with the needles at the doctor's office, and making a speech always seem to make the list.

Many think such fears are silly. I've been flying airplanes for many years, and some say I make a fair speech, too. Both of these acts have brought me moments of fear, but with training and practice there is not much fear anymore.

The fear of needles, I'm told, is just in your mind. This may be true, but I still break out in a sweat and even feel a little faint when I see the nurse coming to give me a shot or draw blood. I remember more about "shot days" in the U.S. Army than my combat training there. In basic training, the old soldiers (the ones who started training two weeks before my company, Company M, 1st ITR Camp Gordon) seemed happy to tell stories about the corkscrew needles that were to be put in the new recruits.

The truth was that on "shot" day you walked through a door, and a medic was on each side of the door. They usually gave two shots in one arm and one in the other. With some mind training related to the posters displayed nearby, the male trooper generally made it OK. I'm not sure what the WACS thought of when they walked through the door.

You can learn to give yourself some mind training to deal with any fears you might have of making a speech. Your ability to make a speech or presentation might very well be the difference in getting a fast raise or promotion. I've heard some people say, "I don't make speeches. I am in data processing, underwriting, or policy holder services. We leave the speech making to marketing." If that is your feeling, you might reconsider and prepare yourself to capitalize on your ability to present your ideas in a speech when you have the opportunity.

The best training I know for making speeches is in a group called the Toastmasters Club. (Also, if your high school or college offers a speech course, take it.) Your first speech in the Toastmasters Club will call for you to stand and tell your name, where you live, something about your family, where you went to school or college, and where you work. I have seen many people do this in such a wonderful way. They did not realize they could even stand without breaking out in a sweat, feeling faint, or having their knees knock.

At each meeting of the Toastmasters Club, you are given what is known as a "table topic." You stand and talk for one minute on an assigned subject. The subject might be "why you feel it is all right to turn right on a red light." You will find yourself telling of the importance of stopping first, looking in all directions, and keeping your line of traffic moving. You will be expressing your thoughts and feelings. You will soon be doing a five-to-fifteen minute speech, a book report, a serious speech, a humorous speech, or a presentation on a technical subject.

Even though you may be in data processing or another technical department and spend much of your time in the technical part of your company, you still need to be prepared to give speeches. You likely will be asked to give a presentation on what your new hardware or software will do for the company. The speech may be to department managers, the executive committee, or the board of directors. You may have butterflies. Some of the great speechmakers of all time will tell you they have butterflies. "Just keep them flying in formation" is my advice.

Most good speakers will write their speech and then make an outline. When you write your own speech, just keep in mind the idea you want to present. You can go back after your speech is on paper and correct the grammar or rearrange a sentence or paragraph. Too, use all the visuals you feel necessary. Visuals of the product and visuals of the numbers and graphs always seem to make a big impression.

When the presentation is complete, your ideas may receive comments like, "Very interesting," "Something to think about and consider," "We'll let you know," or just a plain "thank you." What is really important is the positive impression you leave in the minds of the corporate executives, trustees, or customers. Some remarks will come later, such as that you are really "sharp" or "great on your feet." People may ask, "How long has she or he been with the company? I want to hear more of her or his ideas. She or he is going places with this company or organization."

If you get the decision-makers making those kinds of statements about you and your work, you are well on your way to receiving a pay raise or promotion without asking. Sometimes it only takes one five- or ten-minute presentation. So be prepared.

37

ASK FOR HELP; DECLARE AN EMERGENCY

If you need help in your vocation or your personal life, ask for help. You don't have to know all the answers; just know when to ask.

Use the skills and interests you have to network, build contacts, and entertain. Use your special skills to help others. Much of your success will depend on the people you meet. I have many friends who are doctors, dentists, and lawyers. For many years, I thought patients and clients just flooded their offices. Most will tell you that in their early career they used networking, just as we in the business community do.

Some in our town accuse me of being the best in our community at "working a room" at a Chamber of Commerce meeting or at other group meetings in our community. This accusation embarrassed me some, but I started watching the bankers and saw they were doing the same thing. Since they keep the money in their bank, pay you little to keep it, and charge you a lot when you want to borrow some of it, they must know something.

"Working a room" fits in with what some people call *networking*. The goal is to meet people and make the best possible impression on them for your organization, product, or service.

Some people who really want to meet others, just as you do, might try to make a bad joke by asking what you are "running for" as you go about meeting people. Don't let them get you down. Do it in good taste, but keep meeting people and remembering their names. When you get back to your office or home, drop them a note. (See the section, "Use 'the Power of the Pen.'")

Remember, when you are networking and meeting people you are doing so because you want to know them as a person and not because of what you can gain or get from them. Be sincere, and keep meeting people.

Recently, a new college president moved to our town. Since I was one of the first persons to meet him and his wife, he had lots of questions. I told him of one of the best-qualified financial planners in our town. He became a client of the planner. I told him of my dentist. He and his family are now patients of that dentist. He is a private pilot, and much of his time is spent flying or driving to take care of college business. I introduced him to a partnership where he now has an interest in the plane. His efforts have been greatly multiplied by the time he saves.

Another couple recently joined our company and wanted to buy a house. They wanted to meet a good real estate person. I told them of one I liked and also a banker who makes a special effort to help people finance a home. They told me later that they had talked with both the real estate agent and the banker and that they were on their way toward being in a new home of their own. I know a house is a house and it takes a lot of living to make a home. They are excited, though, and it is already home to them.

All the people you meet and know can become resources for helping others. Remember that it's a compliment to people for you to want to meet them and know their name and their business or profession. You are making a new friend by asking about their home town and their family. Just meet and listen, not meet and talk. It might be that they are more interested in telling about their home town. It may take them some time to get excited about their new move. The truth is that they may have moved to your town just to keep their job.

We started this section talking about asking for help. Maybe your most important time is spent giving help. Asking for help and giving help are closely related.

Recently, my wife Carolyn and I were flying a private plane from Rome, Georgia, to Richmond, Virginia, to attend a meeting. I soloed in May, 1956, when I was in the army at Fort Rucker, Alabama. After my tour of duty, I returned to the business world.

I use general aviation aircraft for both business and pleasure. I don't have many war stories. You don't need to fly much with those who do. I get from A to B fairly quickly, take care of business, and go home. Many of my friends tell me they like to fly with me because I have flown long enough to have gray hair. Someone once said there are lots of bold pilots, but not many old bold pilots.

The trip by small plane from Rome, Georgia, to Richmond, Virginia, gave an opportunity both to ask for help and to give help. We were at 9000 feet with a ground speed of 200 mph in a Cessna 182RG. We departed Rome and contacted Atlanta Center, which keeps you on a big radar screen. The center follows your flight path, advising you of other aircraft, weather, altimeter setting, and other information. In addition to your own instruments and your own eyes, the center is also watching out for you and helping to keep the flight path safe. (By the way, no matter what you might have heard or read, our nation has the best air traffic control system in the world.)

As the flight progressed, Atlanta Center handed us off to Greensboro approach, then back to Atlanta Center, and then to Washington Center. Things were going well. The engine was giving a constant hum, and Carolyn was completing her last thirty minutes of sleep.

Pilots are taught to scan their instruments, trust their instruments, look for other traffic, and always look for a safe place to land if necessary. Our plane will glide about one mile for each 1000 feet of altitude, and so at 9000 feet we could glide nine miles to an airport.

Washington Center had given us the wind and altimeter setting at Richmond International. We were about twenty miles south of Petersburg, Virginia, and I knew shortly we would be given instructions to start our descent to Richmond International. As I scanned the engine instruments, I saw that the oil pressure needle had moved out of the green by the width of one needle. When the oil pressure needle moves out of the green, it means very little or no oil is getting to the engine. It's like very little or no blood is going to your heart.

Now it was time for forty years of flying either to bring immediate panic or to bring to mind what I had been taught to do.
Only a week earlier, I was in a meeting in Savannah, Georgia,
when a co-worker turned pale and his knees buckled. I helped
him to the ground and said to others in the group to give me
some help. In about five seconds, one of the best-looking women
I have ever seen pushed the crowd back and said, "I am a nurse."
She was like a drill sergeant for about thirty seconds, giving com-
mands, checking my friend's pulse, taking off his tie, unbut-
toning his shirt, and putting an ice pack on his head. Finding out
about his low blood sugar, she gave him a piece of sweet candy to
put in his mouth. In the six-to-eight minutes required for the
medics (911) to arrive, she already had him back in this world
and well on his way to feeling better. I called for help, and she
responded. It was great to see a real pro at work.

Now it was my time to ask for help and for someone to give the
help. I said, "Washington Center, this is Cessna 7586X-ray. I have
just lost oil pressure out of the green. What is the nearest airport?"

The reply came back, "Blackstone Airport, 6 miles at one
o'clock." That was 30 degrees right of my heading. Washington
Center continued, "7586X-ray, are you declaring an emergency?"

"86 X-ray, that is affirmative. Does Blackstone have a control
tower?"

"Affirmative."

At this time, I did not realize Blackstone was a military base. In
a period of three or four minutes, Washington Center advised the
Blackstone Army Tower of the emergency, the Army advised their
civil service fire department, military police, and others who
needed to know.

I reduced the power for a quick descent. The steady hum of
cruise power went to approach power, and Carolyn went from a
catnap to being fully awake. I assured her everything was OK and
we would be on the ground shortly. Descending from 9000 feet, I
circled the airport one time, put the landing gear down, and
noticed that the tires had a good bath of oil. The power reduction
caused the oil pressure needle to move back into the green, and so

I knew it was OK to keep the engine running. We were the center of attention, with all the emergency equipment "standing by."

The Blackstone Military Tower gave the instruction, "7586X cleared to land."

A military helicopter called and said, "We have a group of six helicopters ready for landing but will stand by for the emergency."

The landing was one of my better ones, and we taxied to near the control tower, parked, and deplaned. It's not everyday you are greeted by military police, fire trucks, and emergency equipment.

The mechanic checked the problem. A small one-inch seal behind the vacuum pump had failed, and most of the oil was gone from the engine. Only three quarts remained. That three quarts kept the engine alive and got us safely on the ground. A mechanic from Petersburg, Virginia, made the repairs. One of the fire truck drivers had an aunt in Rome, and the control tower operator was from Indianapolis, where we had lived for a few years. We had lunch with the control tower operator and bought enough pizza for the other four tower operators. You will find that when you put people number one you make friends, whether with a flat tire, a lost puppy, or an airplane repair. People love to help people.

We had a good meeting in Richmond, and the repair bill by Performance Aviation from Petersburg was extremely fair. The flight back to Rome three days later was safe and uneventful.

When I returned, I wrote the Commander of Blackstone Army Base a letter, thanking him for the leadership and training given his troops and the professional courtesy extended us. We also wrote the same kind of thank-you letter to the Director of Air Traffic Control at Washington Center. I told her my wife Carolyn (a non-pilot) wanted her to have a special thank-you for the training and leadership she had given her controllers. Our only disappointment was that we did not get to meet her and her controller in person.

I didn't know who the controller in Washington was who helped us to a safe landing, but I gave the date and time of the help needed. Also, the military made a complete report of all persons involved.

I'm not sure we record as much detail in personnel files in the business world as the military and civil service do. I hope that copies of my letter to the Commander and to the Director of Air Traffic will be made part of each person's permanent file for professional service rendered.

Shortly after I wrote the thank-you notes, I received a phone call from a young man who identified himself as the Washington Center controller on duty when I had my emergency. He wanted to thank me for the letter to his supervisor. He also extended a personal invitation for my wife and me to join him for a personal tour of Washington Center. Don't forget "the power of the pen," and don't hesitate to ask for help when you need it.

38

WHEN TROUBLE COMES, KNOW WHERE TO GET HELP

It's not *if* trouble comes, but *when* trouble comes. The secret to your mental, physical, or financial health when trouble comes will be in how well you are prepared to handle it and whether you know where to get help when you need it.

My best advice is, "Don't try to handle it alone." Get the best professional help you can afford. It might surprise you to know that often the best help is not very expensive.

If it is a personal problem, talk to one or two of your best friends, not more than three. I am sure you have heard that you should not tell your problems to *all* your friends and neighbors. The reason is that

• ONLY 25% REALLY CARE AND WANT TO HELP YOU

- ANOTHER 25% ARE GLAD IT'S YOU, AND NOT THEM, WHO HAS
  THE PROBLEM

- AND 50% REALLY DON'T WANT TO HEAR!

Someone once said, "If you think 'nobody knows the troubles I've seen,' you've never lived in a small town." Still, if you feel lonely, feel negatively, or feel no one cares much about you any more, get help from someone.

Many people know how to make a living but not how to make a life. Some think you cannot have both. I hope this book is giving you an idea or two that will help you make both a good living and a good life.

Most of us have two kinds of problems—big problems and little problems. The little ones we can usually handle, by

- GETTING UP AND GOING TO WORK

- SLOWING DOWN INSTEAD OF BEING ASKED TO PAY A TRAFFIC
  TICKET

- PAYING THE WATER AND ELECTRIC BILLS INSTEAD OF GET-
  TING THE WATER AND ELECTRICITY CUT OFF

- TELLING YOUR MOTHER-IN-LAW YOU KNOW HOW TO RAISE
  HER GRANDCHILDREN

- TELLING YOUR FATHER-IN-LAW IF HE WILL TAKE CARE OF
  YOUR MOTHER-IN-LAW, YOU WILL TAKE CARE OF HIS
  DAUGHTER

- TELLING YOUR CO-WORKER TO STOP HUMMING AT HIS DESK
  OR YOU WILL START SINGING AT YOURS

I have the list started, and now you may add to it.

Now for the big troubles or problems. Knowing how you will react when trouble comes and knowing that reaction is normal should provide some comfort to you. The people who have studied our reactions to major troubles or problems sum it up in five stages:

1. DISBELIEF AND SHOCK

2. DENIAL

3. ANGER

4. DEPRESSION

5. RECOVERY

The big problem is when we need a professional to help. We sometimes may need a professional to help with the little problems, too, to keep them from becoming big problems. Here are some suggestions about where you can get help.

- IF IT'S A PERSONAL PROBLEM, CALL A CLOSE FRIEND, A DOCTOR, OR A MINISTER. IT'S OK TO GET A SECOND OPINION.

- IF IT'S A HEALTH PROBLEM, CALL YOUR DOCTOR. IT'S OK TO GET A SECOND OPINION.

- IF IT'S A LEGAL PROBLEM, CALL YOUR LAWYER. IT'S OK TO GET A SECOND OPINION. WHEN IT'S OVER, YOU MIGHT NOT HAVE ANY MONEY, BUT YOU PROBABLY WON'T BE IN JAIL.

- IF IT'S A SPIRITUAL PROBLEM, CALL YOUR MINISTER OR CHAPLAIN.

- IF IT'S A FINANCIAL PROBLEM, CALL YOUR INSURANCE AGENT, BANKER, STOCK BROKER, OR CPA, OR CALL A MEETING OF YOUR PERSONAL BOARD OF DIRECTORS.

The top three major problems have been listed as

- LOSS OF A PERSON YOU LOVE, THROUGH DEATH OR DIVORCE

- LOSS OF YOUR HEALTH OR THE HEALTH OF SOMEONE YOU LOVE

- LOSS OF A JOB YOU LOVE, OR ANOTHER MAJOR FINANCIAL LOSS

When any of these three touches your life, remember the five stages that people go through as they deal with troubles. Remembering them and perhaps seeking help from other people will enable you to get through the times when trouble comes.

39

KEEP YOUR PERSONNEL FILE CURRENT

Be sure to keep your personnel file current. If you have a personnel director or immediate supervisor who keeps your file up-do-date, great. If not, make copies of everything good you have done, and put them in your personnel file. Be sure to include information on community service awards, professional organizations, computer courses, Toastmaster training, continuing education courses, and additional training in trade school, high school, and/or college.

Companies are merging and buying and selling other companies as never before. The president, manager, or supervisor with whom you worked closely for many years may have retired, transferred, or just plain quit. Your mentor may be gone. So keep your personnel files up to date.

Last evening as you were leaving your day of work, the folks up on the forty-second floor could have been going through the personnel files to see who should be the new manager or supervisor on the fourth floor. They could have been looking to see whom they want to call up tomorrow at 10:30 a.m. for a career re-adjustment. Your personnel file could be the door-opener for your next pay raise or promotion. Only one positive note of interest by the right person can keep you moving up, not out. Check your file today. *Do it now.*

Part IV.

SPECIFIC SITUATIONS

40

Civil Servant

Very few people in the business world know as much about promotions, levels of positions, and how you move up the ladder than the civil servant. The business world could learn a lot from the civil service system. If you are a civil service employee or civil service administrator, you probably know more about budgeting, record keeping, documentation, and employee benefits than most.

My father was a farmer, and my mother spent most of her adult years as a homemaker. The last twenty years of her life, though, she worked in a federal community action program. The program helped people learn to support themselves and have balanced meals.

My mother had little personal time except on Sunday. Even then, about the only personal time she had was for Sunday School and church. She spent the rest of the time away from her job in taking care of her family. So, in her busy life, in addition to loving her work, she loved the federal holidays. Don't forget the red letter days yourself; you deserve them.

I have always admired the civil service rating system, which goes from GS-2 through GS-18. If you have not had time to look at it lately, you might like to take a look. Compare the salary of a GS-5 or GS-6 to that of a GS-10 or GS-11. In a lifetime of work, there is a big difference in what you can earn for yourself and your family.

The opportunity for a raise within a rating in the civil service system is very important. So, you might like to study all the levels and prepare yourself for the rungs on the raise or promotion ladder.

My research revealed to me two important factors. These factors apply whether you're in the civil service system or in the corporate world. First, prepare for the job you have and prepare for the next level. Take the necessary training, go back to school if necessary, and in each assignment have someone in your corner.

Second, be sure to help your supervisor achieve whatever his or her objective is. If you will do this, your supervisor is more likely to take care of you. Your job is to complete the task at hand in a positive and friendly way. No greater words can be spoken by your supervisor about you than that you are a team player, that you are focused, that you go the second mile, and that you are positive, creative, and dependable. This applies whether you're under civil service or in the corporate world.

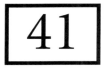

Ph.D.s, Too!

My initial plan for this book was to help young men and women in entry-level and middle-management positions. I wanted the ideas and suggestions, based on my many years of management in the workplace, to help young people overcome feelings of intimidation, fear of rejection, and negative thoughts about themselves. I wanted to help them have a positive feeling about themselves and their worth to the company or organization they served.

I felt that people with a good college education would certainly have the confidence necessary to face up to their own company, school system, college, or university. Why should anyone with as much education as a Ph.D. ever feel intimidated to discuss his or her own advancement with another person? My research revealed that formal education had very little to do with professionals taking charge of their own careers, though. Discussing their financial future seemed a little embarrassing even for some people with high levels of education.

For a time, I served on the board of trustees of one of the finest colleges in the country. Through this service I was selected to serve on the board of the Independent Colleges and Universities in our state. Usually the board was made up of the college president and a business or professional person representing each college or university. Hearing these college presidents talk about their goals and aspirations for their individual colleges or universities was one of my finest hours.

Most of the college presidents came from humble beginnings and then worked hard to reach the top of their professions. I could not believe a teacher, professor, or staff person would not feel comfortable talking to one of these presidents.

As time passed, it seemed that it was not necessarily the person but the position that led to the feeling of uncomfortableness. I soon learned that people with all levels of education need and want information on how to get a raise or promotion without asking. Most people—even Ph.D.s—find it more comfortable helping others than discussing their own financial future.

42

OUR SCHOOLS

Teaching is one of the most important professions in our society. Why has it taken so long even to talk about money for our teachers? We could blame it on the administration, the superintendent of education, or the school board. The blame, however, is on us, the public. We just have not had our values in the right place.

My research revealed that our teachers have the most formal education in the history of our country. They have the ability to teach. They spend hours preparing to teach. In addition to teaching, they must maintain control of the classroom and answer to the principal, the superintendent of education, and the school board.

Each school system needs a program in place for fair compensation and promotion. For this kind of work, the pay needs to be top salary.

When I was discussing pay with one public school teacher, she said, "My raises depend on the state legislature. Isn't that depressing?" We the people need to do better.

In addition, we need to give our teachers and administrators the power to control their classroom and school. One parent or one student who decides there is a better way to run the classroom can cause a lot of problems.

I asked a teacher what she expected from the principal. She said, "Backing and support." She must have known what she was talking about because she was named "Teacher of the Year."

In the rural South, our parents never allowed my brother, sister, or me to take issue with the teacher. If we took issue with the teacher, our parents took issue with us when we got home. I never knew how news traveled so fast. In those days we did not have a telephone, and so we always thought the teacher had a carrier pigeon.

MILITARY PROMOTION AND PAY RAISE

We are proud of our military. Most of us served, or we were willing to serve, when our country needed us. In this country those who did not wear the uniform during World War II served in a support position. During a time of war or national crisis, it was not in good taste to even discuss compensation. During

World War II my uncles served for $21 per month, and during the Korean conflict I served for $78 per month.

When I was in the military, a fine sergeant was always telling us how much our country loved us. In addition to the fine monthly income, there were fine warm clothes, good food to eat, a nice bed or tent for sleep, good medical care, and, if no fighting was going on, you could go home in a year.

A young lieutenant was trying to get the soldiers to sign up for government life insurance. A person would have $10,000 sent to his family in case he did not come back from the battle. Only $2.00 per month would be taken from the soldier's paycheck for such fine coverage.

The lieutenant's presentation was finer than any MBA or financial planner could have made. However, no one was stepping forward to take advantage of this fine offer.

The old sergeant said to the young lieutenant, "Let me see if I can explain in a way the troops can understand."

The sergeant's presentation was brief but to the point. He said to the troops, "Listen up. Our fine lieutenant has made you a fine presentation of the $10,000 benefit your family will receive from our country for $2.00 per month. The United States government does not like to lose money. So, who do you think they are going to send to the front lines first? The ones with the $10,000 insurance or those who do not have the $10,000 coverage?"

Most signed up.

I went back to check some of the promotions to general and admiral. In each case there were several people who could have been promoted into those leadership positions. In each case the promotion meant position and power. With both of these came greater financial reward. This was also true in the other ranks. In each case there seem to have been two items of importance that led to the promotion.

One, the person was qualified educationally, had experience and training for the position, and exemplified an excellent quality of leadership. Second, the person had someone in his corner who believed in him.

Most who have served our country in time of peace will tell you the promotions do not come as fast as in wartime. Too, in many cases young men and women are no longer needed in peacetime for a position for which they have been trained. (Note that though the military downsizers saved the government millions of dollars, they did not receive $16 million to do it as some CEOs have.)

Most military people know the importance of time in grade. If you are a sergeant, the regulations say you need so many years as an E-5 before you become an E-6. Or if you are a major you need so many years as a major (usually three or four) before you are eligible for a promotion to lieutenant colonel. Some "time in grade" is very important.

However, in the regulation there is what is known as a "waiver." Many dedicated military people know of the waiver but do not take advantage of it. The waiver is an advantage to the military and also to the military person. If you are a major filling a lieutenant colonel's position or a corporal filling a sergeant's position, the waiver is ideal for you. Your superior officer in a letter of recommendation makes reference to the regulations, to you, to your rank, to your present position, and to the rank the position calls for. A good letter of recommendation to the promotion board could lead to a promotion that could mean thousands of dollars to your career and future promotions. Maybe most importantly, your retirement income benefits greatly.

In the military, people often move many times. Sometimes the only record of your excellent performance is in your military file. Be sure everything you do in a positive way is included in your personal file. It's like a credit file on you. By chance if there is anything negative in your file, get it out when legally possible. One commander may be a free spirit on how you drive, but the next commander may consider a minor traffic violation an indication of a serious lack of good judgment. So keep a clean and positive record. *And don't forget the waiver.*

44

Pay Raise and Promotion in Health Care

The health care field provides an excellent opportunity for a career in which to receive a pay raise or promotion without asking. Education and training are the keys. The field is very good for both males and females. Our society is thinking more about health than ever before. The baby boomers are aging, and the younger folks are big on preventive medicine.

Here's how one young woman moved to the top of the medical profession. She began by studying hard in school and making the best grades possible. She enjoyed going to the hospital with her parents to visit friends and relatives. She noticed some young women in candy-stripe dresses. The young women were delivering flowers, candy, and gifts to the patients. She told her mother she would like to do that as a volunteer. So, not many months passed before she became a volunteer in the hospital. She learned to talk "hospital and doctor talk." Her newfound vocabulary of medical terms was exciting to her.

She next learned of a course at the local community college that would prepare her to become a practical nurse. She was still doing well with her other school work, and her mother encouraged her.

Soon, on weekends after completing the practical nurse course, she was working at the hospital and earning a salary. She loved caring for patients and getting to know them in a personal way. She could not believe she could get paid and enjoy the work so much.

Like most parents, her parents wanted her to get as much education as possible. Since she was near the top of her class at high school graduation, her parents encouraged her to work toward a

Bachelor of Science degree in nursing at the local college. She agreed, but she still wanted to do some work at the hospital. She was seeing more and more how classroom work related to what she would be doing as a registered nurse. She also noticed that her registered nurse friends seemed to be doing all right financially, and they seemed happy and successful. Her determination increased to make the best grades and become the best registered nurse possible.

She graduated toward the top of her class, excited about being a registered nurse the rest of her life. Her income had increased, and she was doing exactly what she wanted to do. Someone has said that true success comes when you love what you do so much you would do it for nothing. As a result of loving your work, you are well-compensated.

One day in the hospital cafeteria, one of her friends told her of a physician's assistant program at the nearby university. Her friend suggested that since she was young and enjoyed studying, this might be a level of health care she would enjoy.

So she enrolled in the physician's assistant course and graduated near the top of her class. She had never asked for a raise, and the paycheck in her new position was unbelievable to her—another raise in pay because of education.

She continued to enjoy her work with the doctors and the patients. She worked with confidence and was very happy. Her friend was proud of her and suggested maybe while she was still fairly young and did not have many financial obligations she might consider medical school. She had taken many of the pre-med courses and done well. Her parents were not wealthy, but they agreed they would help her financially to attend medical school if that was what she wanted to do.

She told her parents she would like to be a doctor. She considered that being a physician would be the ultimate for her career. She jokingly told her parents that the doctors had reserved parking at the hospital and drove cars with names she could not even pronounce.

You are way ahead of me and have guessed the results. She graduated near the top of her class, completed an internship, and became a very fine doctor. She is well respected in her community—and sets her own fees.

She did look up one day during an operation into the eyes of another young doctor. She soon walked down the aisle at her church with him and now rushes from the hospital to the school where her first-grade daughter has the lead role as a Red Cross nurse in the school play.

I asked her, "What do you like best about being a doctor?"

She replied, "Taking care of my patients."

If she meets her friend "the encourager" one more time in the hospital cafeteria, she will probably be Chief of Staff next year or own the hospital!

Education, training, experience, and her desire to achieve and to serve others were the true ingredients to her success. By the way, she does have the shiny car and boat. This young woman became a very successful doctor, but my guess is that she would have been a happy and successful practical nurse, too. Patient care was important to her.

There are many opportunities in health care. Your local library would be a good source of information. Probably your local hospital or friends in the health care field could also help you.

You may enter the medical field as a young person, or you may consider a mid-career change. A couple of years ago there was a young middle-aged woman in our office; she had always wanted to be a registered nurse. Her son was soon to graduate from high school. While she was still working at our company she enrolled in evening classes at our local community college and completed much of the course work. She resigned her administrative position with our company and completed her preparation to become a registered nurse. She now is a very good registered nurse at a local hospital.

You guessed it. She received a nice pay raise and did not ask anyone. Most important, she is doing what she always wanted to do.

There might be some person who has done all the patient care they ever want to do. If so, come on to the business world. We have some excellent administrative positions for you.

It may seem like a long time was required for either of these examples to get to their goal. It took a long time for the woman who became a doctor to move from being a candy striper, to being a practical nurse, to being a registered nurse, to being a physician's assistant, to being an intern, and at last to being a physician.

One big excuse I hear about not doing what a person really wants to do is age.

- I CAN'T STAY IN COLLEGE. I'LL BE 23 WHEN I GRADUATE.

- I CAN'T GO TO MEDICAL SCHOOL. I'LL BE 30 WHEN I GRADUATE.

- I CAN'T BE A REGISTERED NURSE. I'LL BE 45 WHEN I GRADUATE.

- I CAN'T GO BACK AND GET A MASTER'S DEGREE. I'LL BE 50 WHEN I GRADUATE.

- I CAN'T GO BACK TO LAW SCHOOL. I'LL BE 48 WHEN I GRADUATE.

How old will you be if you don't?

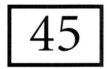

UNIONS

You might get a pay raise without asking just by being a member of a union. The main reason we are discussing organized labor is to help you decide whether you feel you could do better with professional representation for your career. There is a fee for that representation in the form of union dues.

You could debate the pros and cons of unions until Wednesday and still not move very far from zero. Winning or losing such a debate generally depends on whether the person you are talking to favors or opposes unions to begin with.

The other day I was talking to a local resident who had been born and reared in a mill village. His goal as a youth in that village was to get an education, move from the mill village, and not look back. His mother and father worked under a union contract all their working years. As a young man he thought, *No mill village for me and no union.*

Thirty years later, after a successful dental practice, he looked back at his own childhood and at his father's career with the mill as a card-carrying union member. He remembered living through a few strikes, but mostly he remembered the stability of his home life. His mother had supper on the table at a certain time every day. They went to sleep each night with windows up for fresh air and the front door unlocked. The company store was a good place to shop. The village had its own doctor and drug store. The schools were some of the best in the county. Many of the students went to college. The neighbors looked after one another's children, and a "word of correction" from a neighbor was the same as if it came from the parent. Most of all he remembered the ball fields, the swimming pool, and the socials at the church, school, or civic center. In retrospect he thought, *Not a bad way to live.*

Some blame the closing of the textile mill on "the union." Others believe the reason was that cotton was no longer king. Some think the union pushed so hard for wages and benefits that the company was forced to go south of the border for cheaper wages in order to stay competitive in the market place. Arguments for or against unions in any industry generally include such factors as these.

Whatever industry you are in, if you are a card-carrying union worker and still have your job, you are probably happy with the union pay scale and feel certain the company would have never made the wage concession without the encouragement of the union. If you lean toward management's viewpoint, you may have another opinion.

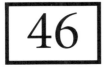

WHERE ARE THE JOBS?

Are you considering a job change or even a career change? This chapter will give you an idea of where to look and what you can expect. This exercise is very useful because it will cause you either to realize what an excellent position you already have or speed up the process of looking for something better.

The first place you might consider visiting is your state employment office. Your state probably will have an office near you. This service can be a great place for resource material and direction. Only about 10% of the jobs come through the state employment office, though, so don't make it your only stop. Other places or persons you should consider are

1. YOUR COLLEGE PLACEMENT OFFICE

2. PROFESSIONAL PLACEMENT COMPANIES (HEADHUNTERS)

3. YOUR OWN AGENT

4. PERSONNEL DIRECTORS OF COMPANIES OR ORGANIZATIONS YOU LIKE

5. PRESIDENT OR EXECUTIVE DIRECTOR OF YOUR UNION

6. LOCAL NEWSPAPER

7. NATIONAL MAGAZINES

8. COMPANY OR ORGANIZATION NEWSLETTERS

9. NETWORKING

10. YOUR PRESENT COMPANY (DON'T LEAVE BEFORE YOU KNOW THE COMPANY'S PLANS.)

11. PRESENT CO-WORKERS

12. FORMER CO-WORKERS

13. TEACHERS OR COLLEGE PROFESSORS

Since you just read this list of thirteen, see whether you can think of thirteen more. After your list is complete, then narrow the list to two or three you want to work on. However, while you are being specific with two or three groups, you might also consider using the shotgun approach. Send your letter and resumé to as many prospective employers as possible to get your name in front of them.

Your state will have information on the job outlook. The job situation in my state, Georgia, has been very good in recent years, and the job outlook continues to look good. In the year 2005, total employment in Georgia is expected to reach more than 4.2 million jobs with more than 72,000 new jobs added each year. Georgia's economy is currently growing faster than the national economy as a whole, with expected job growth of 2.2% per year over the next decade as compared with 1.7% for the United States.[1] As hundreds of young children said to the world during the 1996 Centennial Olympic Games in Atlanta, "Y'all come now."

Industries and occupations grow at varying rates, depending on demand for their products or services and on changes in technology. Job opportunities are also created by workers leaving an occupation to enter another occupation, to return to school, to stay home with children, or to retire, among other reasons.

The following are fourteen occupational "interest areas." These interest areas group together occupations involving similar activities. The largest group of openings is in the business and clerical

---

[1] The source for the statistics in this chapter is the Georgia Department of Labor.

area, with about two-thirds of these in clerical occupations. Large numbers of openings are also expected in the sales and the commercial services interest areas. The smallest number of openings will be in the agriculture/forestry and arts/recreation areas.

The high-demand occupations from 1992 through 2005 are as follows:

INTEREST AREA	PERCENT OF OPENINGS
Business/Clerical	23%
Math/Science/Engineering	3%
Health Services	6%
Community Services	2%
Education	7%
Arts/Recreation	1%
Sales	18%
Protective Services	3%
Commercial Services	19%
Construction	4%
Transportation	4%
Agricultural/Forestry	1%
Mechanics/Crafts	5%
Manufacturing Production	6%

Occupations vary greatly in earning levels. Among the most important factors affecting the wages paid to workers in different occupations is the level of preparation required. Preparation can include college or university education, vocational education or apprenticeship training, on-the-job training, or specific kinds of work experience. Let's consider the annual openings by preparation level required.

1. 48% REQUIRE A HIGH SCHOOL DIPLOMA AND/OR UP TO FOUR YEARS OF EDUCATION BEYOND HIGH SCHOOL, VOCATIONAL TRAINING, OR SPECIFIC WORK EXPERIENCE.

2. 17% REQUIRE A COLLEGE DEGREE OR MORE.

3. 35% HAVE NO SPECIFIC EDUCATION, TRAINING, OR EXPERIENCE REQUIRED.

It's fairly safe to say that the best way to take advantage of the "good life" is through education and training. The American dream usually will come with hard work, education, and training.

CAREER EXPLORATION

If you love your work so much you would do it for no compensation, then you likely will be very successful in your chosen field and will be compensated for your efforts. So choosing the right career is important.

There are several important factors to consider in choosing a career. Some of them are as follows:

• OPPORTUNITY FOR ADVANCEMENT

• HOW YOUR APTITUDES FIT THOSE NEEDED FOR THE OCCUPATION

• WHERE TRAINING IS GIVEN, ITS COSTS, AND FINANCIAL PROSPECTS

- How many workers may be competing for available openings

- Working conditions (hours, indoor or outdoor work, hazards, stress)

- In what industries the occupation is found

- Where jobs are located (city, small town, rural area)

Most jobs will not come to you. You must explore every possibility that sparks your interest.

48

Who Makes the Money? How Much? Are There Openings?

You may check with your state department of labor or department of industry, trade, and tourism to find who makes the money, how much, and where the openings are in your state. Here is a listing of the occupations, annual openings, entry wages, and average wages in my state, Georgia. I hope this list sparks your interest.

If you don't find the job you like in your state, come on to Georgia. We still have plenty of grits if you have not yet acquired the good taste of the "good life." We also have steak, pork, fish, and some good pizza places.

Occupation	Annual Openings	Entry Wage	Average Wage
Accountants & auditors	1,050	$12.40	$16.50
Adjustment clerks	550	$7.95	$9.65
Administrative services managers	170	$14.85	$18.80
Advertising sales agents	150	$9.95	$15.60
Aircraft mechanics	100	$ 8.45	$15.80
Aircraft pilots & flight engineers	140	$16.50	$19.05
Amusement & recreation attendants	350	$5.20	$6.15
Architects	110	$14.90	$21.20
Artists & commercial anists	230	$10.05	$15.45
Automotive body repairers	200	$8.90	$12.15
Automotive mechanics	910	$8.70	$12.05
Bakers	260	$5.50	$7.10
Bank tellers	400	$6.50	$7.50
Barbers	110	$5.95	$6.00
Bartenders	210	$5.15	$5.90
Bill & account collectors	360	$7.20	$9.25
Billing, cost & rate clerks	300	$7.65	$9.05
Bookkeeping & accounting clerks	540	$7 45	$9.20
Brick masons	120	$9.00	$12.45
Brick & stonemason helpers	100	$6.05	$7.90
Bus, truck & diesel engine mechanics	410	$9.00	$11.35
Business services sales agents	310	$11.10	$14.15
Buyers-w'sale & retail (ex. farm prod)	180	$10.55	$19.40
Cabinetmakers & bench carpenters	150	$6.75	$8.90
Carpenters	770	$8.20	$10.95
Carpenter helpers	210	$6.10	$7.50
Cashiers	5,890	$ 4.75	$5.50
Child care workers	1,370	$4.70	$5.40
Civil engineers	220	$14.50	$21.15
Clergy	160	$13.60	$15.95
Communication/transp/util managers	170	$16.05	$20.00
Computerengineers	270	$15.35	$21.60
Computer programmers	640	$12.95	$16.75
Computer programmer aides	130	$ 8.70	$10.65
Concrete & terrazo finishers	140	$7.65	$10.10
Construction managers	260	$15.55	$19.65
Cooks-fast food	1,340	$4.40	$4.80

Occupation	Annual Openings	Entry Wage	Average Wage
Cooks-institution or cafeteria	680	$5.05	$6.00
Cooks-restaurant	1,070	$5.40	$6.85
Cooks-short order	250	$4.70	$5.30
Correction officers & jailers	560	$8.80	$9.50
Cost estimators	160	$13.45	$17.30
Counter & rental clerks	380	$5.00	$5.95
Counter attendants-coffee shop or cafe	760	$4.45	$5.00
Crush/grind/mix machine oprs	110	$9.05	$9.95
Customer service reps-utilities	210	$7.30	$9.50
Data entry keyers	330	$6.90	$8.15
Data processing equipment repairers	190	$9.30	$13.15
Demonstrators, promoters & models	240	$6.45	$8.20
Dental assistants	230	$6.80	$8.80
Dental hygienists	150	$13.05	$15.80
Dentists	110	$26.10	$46.60
Designers (except interior design)	230	$9.55	$13.10
Detectives & investigators (private)	110	$9.20	$11.35
Dining room, cafeteria & bar helpers	630	$4.60	$5.25
Dispatchers (except police, fire & amb)	180	$8.30	$10.75
Drafters	280	$9.80	$12.30
Driver/sales workers	550	$8.55	$11.65
Drywall installers	110	$7.55	$11.05
Education administrators	480	$17.70	$26.30
Electrical & electronic assemblers	280	$6.65	$7.70
Elec. & e'tronic assemblers (precision)	120	$8.75	$10.65
Elec. & e'tronic engineering techs	220	$10.65	$13.55
Electrical & electronic engineers	350	$16.05	$21.80
Electricians	490	$9.40	$13.85
Electrician helpers	180	$6.20	$7.90
Emergency medical technicians	190	$7.70	$9.40
Employment interviewers	120	$8.75	$11.80
Engineering/math/nat'l sciences mgrs	370	$22.75	$28.30
Farm managers	270	N.A.	N.A.
File clerks	340	$5.65	$6.60
Financial managers	660	$20.05	$24.70
Fire fighters	360	$9.10	$10.60

Occupation	Annual Openings	Entry Wage	Average Wage
Flight attendants	180	$7.40	N.A.
Food preparation workers	2,120	$4.75	$5.40
Food prep. & serve - fast food	2,330	$4.60	$5.05
Food servers (outside)	190	N.A.	$5.60
Food service & lodging managers	830	$ 9.50	$13.45
Freight, stock & material handlers	1,700	$6.60	$7.85
Gardeners & groundskeepers	610	$5.60	$6.80
General managers & top executives	3,040	$21.50	$30.00
General office clerks	2,680	$6.50	$7.95
Grader, bulldozer & scraper oprs	120	$7.75	$9.50
Guards	1,210	$5.80	$6.75
Hairdressers & cosmetologists	590	$5.35	$7.15
Hand packers & packagers	990	$6.65	$7.60
HVAC & refrigeration mechanics	280	$8.30	$11.95
Highway maintenance workers	190	$6.30	$7.75
Home health aides	540	$5.15	$5.65
Hosts & hostesses-restaurants	250	$4.85	$5.85
Hotel desk clerks	170	$5.20	$5.90
Human services workers	180	$7.80	$9.15
Industrial engineers	150	$18.35	$22.20
Industrial production managers	170	$21.60	$23.35
Industrial truck & tractor operators	570	$7.85	$9.20
Inspectors & compliance officers	130	$10.95	$13.90
Instructors & coaches-sports	170	$8.00	$10.80
Insulation workers	110	$6.65	$10.55
Insurance adjusters & examiners	220	$11.40	$13.55
Insurance claims clerks	100	$7.40	$9.25
Insurance policy processing clerks	150	$7.80	$8.95
Insurance sales workers	290	$9.65	$14.45
Janitors & cleaners	2,220	$5.35	$6.50
Laundry & drycleaning operators	280	$4.85	$5.45
Lawyers	440	$20.55	$36.65
Legal secretaries	360	$9.65	$12.25
Librarians	150	$11.55	$16.75

Occupation	Annual Openings	Entry Wage	Average Wage
Library assists & bookmobile drivers	130	$5.85	$6.45
Licensed practical nurses	860	$8.70	$10.05
Loan & credit clerks	120	$7.60	$9.05
Machine feeders & offbearers	360	$7.25	$8.10
Machine forming oprs-metal & plastic	100	$8.50	$10.00
Mach. maint mechanics-industrial	300	$10.90	$12.95
Mach. maint. mech.-water/power plant	130	$8.65	$10.85
Machinists	210	$11.45	$13.80
Maids & housekeeping cleaners	660	$4.75	$5.30
Mail clerks (except Postal Service)	210	$6.35	$7.65
Maintenance repairers-general	1000	$7.80	$9.50
Management analysts	280	$15.20	$22.75
Marketing/advertising/pr mgrs.	650	$19.15	$24.35
Meat, poultry, fish cutters & trimmers	720	$6.40	$6.55
Mechanic & repairer helpers	970	$6.65	$7.75
Mechanical engineers	230	$16.35	$20.70
Medical assistants	300	$6.80	$8.25
Medical laboratory technologists	120	$11.25	$14.00
Medical records technicians	110	$6.25	$8.15
Medical secretaries	290	$7.25	$8.95
Medicine & health services managers	220	$15.90	$21.85
Millwrights	110	$16.70	$17.30
Mobile heavy equip mech (ex. engines)	100	$9.40	$11.60
New accounts clerks	100	$7.40	$8.85
Nursery workers	180	$4.35	$5.90
Nursing aides & orderlies	1,450	$4.75	$5.50
Office machine servicers	110	$6.95	$9.15
Offset litho press setters/set-up oprs.	210	$11.55	$13.50
Order clerks-materials & services	300	$7.65	$8.95
Order fillers-sales	320	$6.30	$7.70
Packaging machine operators	130	$8.25	$8.95
Painters & paperhangers	450	$7.70	$10.35
Painting machine operators	110	$8.85	$10.15
Paralegals	180	$9.95	$13.40
Paving/surfacing/tamping equip oprs.	210	$7.45	$9.10

Occupation	Annual Openings	Entry Wage	Average Wage
Payroll & timekeeping clerks	140	$7.60	$9.85
Personnel/training/labor rel. mgrs	270	$17.25	$20.75
Personnel/training/labor rel. specialist	400	$11.80	$14.45
Personnel clerks (except payroll)	170	$8.10	$9.70
Pharmacists	180	$19.40	$22.80
Physical therapists	160	$17.70	$22.50
Physical therapy assistant & aides	120	$5.95	$7.20
Physicians	410	$50.70	$86.55
Plumbers & pipefitters	360	$9.10	$13.75
Plumber & pipefitter helpers	150	$5.75	$7.25
Police patrol officers	410	$9.40	$11.15
Postal mail carriers	290	$16.00	N.A.
Pressing machine oprs.(textiles)	150	$5.10	$6.05
Printing press machine operators	150	$8.95	$10.55
Production & expediting clerks	230	$9.75	$11.75
Prod. inspectors, testers'& graders	270	$7.75	$8.60
Property & real estate managers	240	$12.10	$15.60
Psychologists	110	$12.70	$18.00
Public relations specialists	100	$11.80	$14.65
Purch. agents (ex. w'sale/ret./farm)	140	$11.60	$14.40
Purchasing managers	230	$14.75	$18.45
Radiologic technologists	130	$11.85	$14.70
Real estate sales agents	170	$9.50	$13.30
Receptionists & information clerks	1,090	$6.30	$7.40
Recreation workers	110	$6.65	$8.95
Refuse & recyclables collectors	100	$6.10	$7.40
Registered nurses	1,630	$13.55	$17.40
Respiratory therapists	110	$12.80	$15.10
Sales reps (ex. scientific & retail)	2,030	$12.40	$16.15
Sales reps. (scientific prod ex. retail)	550	$13.60	$18.15
Salespersons-parts	360	$6.85	$9.35
Salespersons-retail	5,130	$5.75	$8.10
School bus drivers	610	$6.35	$6.80
Secretaries (except legal & medical)	2,440	$7.65	$9.80
Securities & financial services sales	220	$12.80	$15.80
Service station attendants	130	$5.25	$6.40

Occupation	Annual Openings	Entry Wage	Average Wage
Sewing machine operators-nongarment	170	$5.95	$8.00
Sheet metal workers	250	$7.25	$12.35
Sheriffs & deputy sheriffs	160	$9.15	$11.45
Shipping, receiving & traffic clerks	1,020	$6.85	$8.25
Social workers	290	$10.65	$12.25
Stock clerks-sales floor	1,300	$4.90	$5.95
Stock clerks-stockroom or warehouse	670	$6.70	$8.65
Supervisors-cleaning & bldg services	120	$6.85	$8.20
Supervisors-clerical workers	1,360	$10.10	$12.80
Supervisors-construction	480	$11.55	$15.10
Supervisors-fire fighting & prevention	110	$11.70	$15.10
Supervisors-helpers & laborers	140	$8.70	$9.80
Supervisors-mech/installers/repairers	470	$11.50	$14.65
Supervisors-police & detectives	160	$11.65	$14.15
Supervisors-prod & operating workers	700	$13.80	$15.75
Supervisors-sales & related workers	2,370	$11.50	$14.45
Sup.-transp.mat'l moving equip. oprs.	160	$10.40	$17.45
Systems analysts	1,340	$15.85	$19.30
Tax preparers	150	$5.55	$7.85
Teacher aides-clerical	440	$5.20	$6.15
Teacher aides-paraprofessional	1,100	$5.55	$6.55
Teachers-elementary school	1,910	$9.90	$13.90
Teachers-kindergarten }	760	$9.90	$13.25
Teachers-preschool		$5.85	$7.30
Teachers-secondary school	1,950	$9.90	$14.70
Teachers-social sciences (college)	130	$10.70	$15.95
Teachers-special education	870	$10.30	$14.15
Teachers-voc education & training	350	$12.15	$15.75
Telemarketers/vendors/outside sales	290	$6.75	$6.75
Textile dyeing machine operators	130	$8.00	$8.40
Textile machine operators	330	$8.05	$8.65
Tire repairers & changers	170	$5.70	$7.05
Travel agents	180	$7.20	$11.45
Truck drivers-heavy	1,910	$9.30	$11.60
Truck drivers-light (incl. delivery)	1,180	$6.85	$8.25
Typists (including word processing)	210	$7.55	$9.20

Occupation	Annual Openings	Entry Wage	Average Wage
Vehicle & equipment cleaners	180	$4.65	$5.60
Vocational & educational counselors	120	$11.15	$15.50
Waiters & waitresses (wages only)	3,550	$3.40	$3.70
Water & waste treatment plant oprs	110	$7.90	$10.05
Welders & cutters	400	$8.75	$10.70
Welfare eligibility workers	140	$6.55	$8.65
Writers & editors	120	$12.30	$16.70

WHERE DO THEY GET THE MONEY?

Did you ever wonder why some of your friends live in fine houses and drive big or sporty-looking cars? how they afford boats or airplanes? how they have lake homes or cabins in the mountains? how they seem always to go on nice vacations in Europe, the Holy Land, the Far East, or—even better—a wonderful vacation in the good ol' USA?

You, though, find yourself eating fast food. You would like to have a dining experience in which the waiter or waitress quotes the "catch of the day" or other special dishes prepared especially for you. You would like to set a fine table with table cloths and more silverware than even Emily knows how to advise you to use. You know there must be something more than fries, shakes, and burgers.

So how do these folks do all the things they do? The simple answer is, "They have more money." The question is, "Where did they get the money?" I've spent most of my career encouraging people to save and protect their assets. But it's also important to find ways to get the money to begin with.

A couple of easy ways to get the "big bundle" are to (1) inherit it or (2) marry it. But the best way and probably the one most will use is "the old-fashioned way"—earn it by working for it.

Perhaps you are saying, "Big deal. We all know that."

That's true. We do. The difference, though, is the amount in the paycheck for the work we do.

The other morning I stopped to help a friend with his car. He had the hood up and had just bumped his head while checking the fan belt. He was kicking the bumper. After a brief hello, he commented that his neighbor was the luckiest guy in the world because he had both "a car and a wife that is working."

Still, rather than looking at a family with two wage-earners, we'll look at a one paycheck family. Let's look at an example of a person who works forty years, from age twenty-five to age sixty-five. Here are two people with the same basic ability and talent but who have a wide range in their earnings.

"HARD LIFE" WORKER

Annual Income	Years of service	Total Life Income
$10,000	40	$400,000
$20,000	40	$800,000
$30,000	40	$1,200,000
$40,000	40	$1,600,000
$50,000	40	$2,000,000
$60,000	40	$2,400,000

"GOOD LIFE" WORKER

Annual Income	Years of service	Total Life Income
$ 15,000	40	$600,000
$ 25,000	40	$1,000,000
$ 35,000	40	$1,400,000
$ 45,000	40	$1,800,000
$ 55,000	40	$2,200,000
$ 65,000	40	$2,600,000

Annual Income	Years of service	Total Life Income
$ 75,000	40	$3,000,000
$ 85,000	40	$3,400,000
$ 95,000	40	$3,800,000
$100,000	40	$4,000,000
$125,000	40	$5,000,000
$150,000	40	$6,000,000
$175,000	40	$7,000,000
$200,000	40	$8,000,000
$225,000	40	$9,000,000
$250,000	40	$10,000,000

Of course, we all know that earnings increase gradually and that most do not earn at the entry level the same as they do in their later years of employment. The secret is to get the amount of pay increased as quickly as possible and to keep the salary growing.

The "hard life" worker often peaks at around $60,000. Review the information and consider what would happen, though, if his or her earnings peaked at an even lower level.

Of course, you may be saying that very few people start at $100,000 per year. That is correct. Here again, though, the idea is to reach a higher income as quickly as you can.

Recently I met a young couple who met in professional school. They fell in love and married. When they graduated and began their careers, they began at a high level in their earnings. Because of how difficult their financial situation had been in professional school, they were amazed by their earnings and their earning potential. They were both very grateful to live in a country that provided such a wonderful opportunity for earnings as they provided needed services in their work.

Part V.

LESSONS FOR WHEN YOU'VE MOVED UP

50

MANAGEMENT STYLES

People tend to have many complaints about their supervisors. The fact is, though, that you will probably be helped as much by the things your supervisor does that you do not like as by the things you do like. So, in your success notebook, make a list of the things your supervisor does that you do not like. Then, when you are promoted, do not do the things that you disliked. Also, put in your success notebook the things your supervisor did that you liked. When you become supervisor, do those things that you liked.

You may think this is just a way of making lemonade when life hands you a lemon. It also, however, will provide a win for you later even though things might not be so good immediately.

Recently I saw a card that read, "It's hard to soar with eagles when you have to work with the turkeys." That statement is good for a chuckle, but personally I do not like it. It's really a put-down of other people. To get the pay raise and the promotion that you deserve, you will want to lift people up. Learn to be specific in your praise of individuals and your company.

In management it often is not a matter of a right way or a wrong way, but rather a certain management style. The experienced leader and manager will use many means to exercise his or her influence to stimulate those he leads to productive efforts. The following are five of the most typical styles, ranging from highly leader-centered to highly group-centered.

Telling

In the "telling" style, the leader identifies a problem, considers alternative solutions, chooses one of them, and then tells his or her followers what they are to do. He may or may not consider what he believes the group members will think or feel about the decision. Clearly, however, the group members do not participate directly in the decision-making. Coercion may or may not be used or implied.

Persuading

As with the previous style, the leader who uses the style of persuading makes the decision without consulting the group. However, instead of simply announcing his decision, he tries to persuade the group members to accept it. He describes how his decision fits both the interests of the organization and the interests of the group members.

Consulting

In the consulting style, the leader gives the group members a chance to influence the decision from the beginning. He or she presents a problem and relevant background information and then asks members for their ideas on how to solve it. The leader may give his or her tentative solution.

In effect, the group is asked to increase the number of alternative actions to be considered. The leader then selects the solution he regards as most promising.

Joining

In the joining style, the leader participates in the discussion as just another group member and agrees in advance to carry out whatever decision the group makes. The only limits placed on the group are those the leader's superiors have given. (Many research and development teams make decisions this way.)

Delegating

The leader using the delegating style defines a problem and the boundaries within which it must be solved. Then the leader turns the problem over to the group to work out a solution that makes sense. He agrees to support their solution as long as it fits within the boundaries.

Which Is Best for You?

Maybe each of these methods will be helpful to you, depending on the project or task at hand. Maybe you will use a mixture of all five styles, depending on the group you are leading.

51

Motivating Your Staff

You may find that as you move up the ladder you will have a few—or many—people who will report to you. When that happens, your success will no longer be based solely on your own individual efforts but on the efforts of the people you supervise. You will want to consider putting into practice the following ways of motivating the employees on your staff:

- USE APPROPRIATE METHODS OF REINFORCEMENT. THAT IS, BASE ALL REWARDS ON PERFORMANCE, PROVIDE INDIVIDUAL-IZED REINFORCEMENT, AND REINFORCE AS SOON AS POSSIBLE.

- AVOID THREATS AND PUNISHMENTS.

- RECOGNIZE ACCOMPLISHMENTS.

- PROVIDE YOUR STAFF WITH AS MUCH FLEXIBILITY AND AS MANY DECISION-MAKING RESPONSIBILITIES AS POSSIBLE.

- PROVIDE SUPPORT WHEN NEEDED.

- PROVIDE RESPONSIBILITY ALONG WITH ACCOUNTABILITY. REMEMBER THAT IF YOU *EXPECT,* YOU MUST *INSPECT.*

- ENCOURAGE PERSONAL GOAL-SETTING.

- KEEP PEOPLE INFORMED ABOUT HOW THEIR WORK RELATES TO YOUR PERSONAL GOALS AND TO YOUR COMPANY'S GOALS.

- CLARIFY YOUR EXPECTATIONS, AND MAKE SURE THAT PEOPLE UNDERSTAND THEM.

- PROVIDE AN APPROPRIATE LEVEL OF REWARDS WHILE PER-MITTING PEOPLE TO EXPERIENCE THE PERSONAL SATISFAC-TION OF A JOB WELL DONE.

- TREAT PEOPLE AS INDIVIDUALS.

- PROVIDE IMMEDIATE FEEDBACK.

- AVOID NEGATIVE EVALUATIVE FEEDBACK WITHOUT PRO-VIDING INFORMATIONAL FEEDBACK.

- LOOK FOR AND HELP TO ELIMINATE BARRIERS TO INDIVIDUAL ACHIEVE MENT.

- EXPECT ACHIEVEMENT, AND EXHIBIT CONFIDENCE IN OTHERS.

- BE INTERESTED IN AND KNOWLEDGEABLE ABOUT EACH PERSON WHOM YOU SUPERVISE.

- PROVIDE EACH INDIVIDUAL WITH OPPORTUNITIES TO BE SUCCESSFUL OR TO BE A SIGNIFICANT PART OF A SUCCESS.

- ENCOURAGE INDIVIDUALS TO PARTICIPATE IN MAKING DECI-SIONS THAT AFFECT THEM.

- ESTABLISH A CLIMATE OF TRUST AND OPEN COMMUNICATION.

- MINIMIZE THE USE OF STATUTORY POWER—YOUR AUTHORITY, IN OTHER WORDS.

- POINT OUT THE SIGNIFICANCE AND RELEVANCE OF EACH PERSON'S WORK TO THE WHOLE.

- LISTEN TO AND HANDLE COMPLAINTS BEFORE THEY GET OUT OF HAND.

- POINT OUT IMPROVEMENTS IN PERFORMANCE.

- DEMONSTRATE YOUR OWN MOTIVATION THROUGH YOUR BEHAVIOR AND ATTITUDE.

- CRITICIZE BEHAVIOR, NOT PEOPLE.

- GIVE A GREATER AMOUNT OF POSITIVE FEEDBACK TO THOSE TO WHOM YOU HAVE TO GIVE THE MOST SUPERVISION.

- ENCOURAGE PEOPLE TO "TRY SOMETHING DIFFERENT" AND TO ACCEPT NEW CHALLENGES.

- DON'T ELIMINATE ANXIETY. INSTEAD, KEEP IT AT A LEVEL THAT PROVIDES SOME PRESSURE WITHOUT CAUSING DISORI-ENTATION.

- MAKE SURE THAT EFFORT PAYS OFF IN RESULTS.

- BE CONCERNED WITH BOTH SHORT-TERM AND LONG-TERM MOTIVATION.

52

CRITICISM

Criticism is criticism. Recently I heard a lecture on the value of constructive criticism. If you are giving the criticism, it may seem constructive. However, if you are receiving the "constructive" criticism, it is just plain criticism.

Most good managers find a way to correct a situation through teaching. The Army used to call it a critique. How could we have done this differently? What are the alternatives? Which alternative produces the best results?

I teach a few people each year to fly airplanes. The teaching technique we use to teach flying is to

- DEMONSTRATE THE MANEUVER TO THE STUDENT

- OBSERVE THE STUDENT DO THE MANEUVER

- CORRECT THE PART OF THE MANEUVER THAT NEEDS CORRECTING

- DEMONSTRATE, OBSERVE, AND CORRECT AGAIN

Teaching flying has come a long way since the "good old days." In the old days, the louder an instructor screamed at the students, the better instructor he or she was considered to be. Today that kind of instructor would last about one lesson.

In high school and college teaching, the professors soon learn the best method is to make the subject interesting, and the student will learn. Too, most good teachers and business managers know they should always attack the problem and not the person.

Of course, if there is dishonesty, fraud, or an act that would cause harm to other individuals or to the organization, it is time to take immediate action. Constructive criticism or any kind of criticism would be in order. However, you need to use your best management skills in such cases. It's best to get your legal staff involved before you start shooting from the hip.

53

I Won't Tell

Several years ago I had the responsibility and opportunity to review with the president an employee's excellent qualities. She was competent and bright, as you'll soon see. We'll call her Jane.

Jane worked in a clerical position at that time. She since has made excellent progress and moved up in the organization to a middle management position. I have come to realize that she had more insight and depth than many of us, primarily because of her honesty.

The president and I reviewed all the pluses and maybe one or two minuses of this employee. The president asked me to review the pluses, thank her, commend her, and congratulate her for the excellent contribution she had made to the company during the past year. He also asked me to make a couple of suggestions to her on how she might improve and move the two minor minuses to the plus side of her personal assets.

The president told me to advise Jane that we were proud of her and that the company was going to give her a little raise. Also, he asked me to remind her that we do not discuss our raises with other company employees. (Even though this may be a company policy, always remember the grapevine is very reliable.)

I went to great lengths to follow the president's instructions. When I met with Jane, I made a very positive and what I thought was an exciting annual review. I told Jane, "We thank you, we appreciate you, we commend you, and we are proud of you."

I told her the company was going to give her a little raise, but that the president had asked that she not mention it to her co-workers. Jane looked at the little raise on her review. Then she said she would not mention the little raise to anyone because she was as ashamed of it as he was!

54

Dumb Things Smart Managers Do

Most people who have ever managed one person or ten thousand people will admit they've made mistakes. Many times their mistakes have nearly destroyed their management career. More often than not, those very mistakes when corrected have leapfrogged them into high positions of management. I have made my share of mistakes, and I'm sure you probably have made one or two.

One of the biggest mistakes new managers make is in thinking there is only one management style. Some managers out there are real lulus, but some of the management styles you dislike the most may help you the most. If you will not prejudge people, you can learn a lot from almost all of them.

A person should be fairly competent when he or she gets out of college. At least they have the basic skills to get them started. They should start immediately working on their people skills, and they should also plan to keep up-to-date with their technical skills. Most professions require continuing education to keep up-to-date with technical skills. Our colleges and universities also offer special courses or graduate programs to help people keep current in their business or profession.

Anyone with any leadership at all can do a good job at being a manager. Don't think that just the outgoing, goal-setting, top achievers can become managers. In addition to your own list of qualities for being a good manager, please consider the following:

- BE A GOOD LISTENER. In sales organizations many years ago, we used to look for people who were good talkers. Today we look for people who are good listeners.

- TAKE TIME TO TALK TO PEOPLE. Several months ago, I told one of our vice presidents we had an agent who would be bringing us a $15,000 check. He said to me, "You visit with him. I have my Monday morning telephone calls to make." I went back to my office thinking that must be the dumbest statement I had ever heard. We get lots of $1000, $2000, $3000, $4000, and $5000 checks for our product, but we don't get lots of $15,000 checks. If you are too busy to visit with a customer, agent, or employee who brings you any kind of check for your product or service, then you are too busy. As I was thinking these things, I looked down the hall, and the vice president looked like the road runner on Saturday morning television as he came toward my office. He said, "I am too busy if I don't have time to accept a $15,000 check!" I thought to myself, "The 'smart pills' are working today."

- LEARN SOMETHING ABOUT TAXES. If you plan to achieve anything financially in the business world, in your profession, or in your personal life, you need to know something about taxes. If you know anything about taxes, anyone you talk with will really be excited to hear what you have to say. Most folks know how to gripe about taxes, but if you can give a few ideas on how to reduce income taxes, estate taxes, sales taxes, or other taxes, you will be more popular than you've ever dreamed you would be. Don't suggest a tax evasion idea, or you will be as unpopular as a scam artist at an IRS convention. There are some great tax attorneys, CPAs, and financial planners who will give you a shoe box of good tax ideas to use and to share with others.

- LEARN SOMETHING ABOUT INTEREST. If you guide the people you manage so that a sizable part of their income will not go to make interest payments, then they will believe you are providing excellent leadership. You will be in demand as a "leader and manager." I call it the "Aunt Bess" method of personal financial management. Aunt Bess said quietly, "I don't pay interest; I receive it." So, remember the way to financial security is, *people at work and money at work.* So, you must work and make your money work for you if financial security is your goal.

- SINCE PEOPLE WILL SOMETIMES PREJUDGE YOU, KEEP SHARP IN YOUR APPEARANCE AND YOUR ATTITUDE. Buy the best clothes you can afford, but don't over-dress. Quality in the business and professional world is always in order. Two quality suits are better than five of the "cheap-os." Keep neat. Folks look at shoes, so keep them shined and with good heels on them. If the boss is a former military person, your shoes will be checked before your latest computer printout or other technical contribution. Be sharp. Furthermore, if you are going for an interview, you will not impress the prospective employer if you are blowing nicotine. In addition, in your attitude, accentuate the positive and eliminate the negative. If you associate with negative people, they will tend to bring you down to their level. I am not as hard on negative people as I used to be, though. I borrow money from them, and they don't expect it back.

- CONTROL YOUR EMOTIONS. One moment of uncontrolled emotion can destroy a career. It does not make sense to "blow up" or offend someone just because you could not control your temper. Show emotion when you want to show kind feelings toward family or friend or co-worker, but make the management decisions with your mind.

- DO THE BEST YOU CAN IN THE JOB YOU ARE ASSIGNED. Some people want to do everybody's job except their own. The happiest people are the people who take care of their own jobs. Let the president be the president; let the lawyer do the lawyering; let the accountant do the accounting; let the supervisor supervise; let the pilot be the pilot; let the preacher preach; and you do your job.

- SUPPORT YOUR COMPANY OR ORGANIZATION. The happiest people are the people who really support their company or organization. People have a tendency to talk negatively about their company or organization. If you are really unhappy with your employer, you should leave. Find a job where you are happy. One of the saddest things is to spend twenty-five or thirty years with an organization, retire, and then look back and say, "I hated every day I was there."

- DON'T MISTREAT EMPLOYEES. I am unhappy with some companies that will work a person for twenty-five years and the last one or two years of employment treat him or her like a second-class citizen. When this happens, the employee hates the company or at least the way he or she was treated. That is dumb. What is smart is to have a very strong organization of retired employees. Properly supported and managed, the retired group will help your company take giant steps into the twenty-first century. Your present employees are not dumb. They know if you treat your retired employees like "bums," it will only be a matter of time until they will be treated the same way. A board of directors that allows their officers and managers to mistreat employees should be bull-whipped at high noon in front of the courthouse. This does not worry me too much because directors, officers, and managers who do not look after their company's people will soon not have a company to manage. Progressive management is to be admired, and mistreating of employees in the name of progress is just plain dumb. The bottom-line ink will go to a bright red.

- DON'T GLOAT OVER THE POWER TO FIRE. If there is a serious conflict in management style or a difference in opinions that adversely affects the company, you may have to replace a person. However, a manager makes a mistake gloating over the power to fire.

- HELP OTHER PEOPLE. Good managers take pride in helping other people. Good managers are always in the people development business. Many people think you get to the top by stepping on other people, but success comes from lifting other people.

- GET ALONG WITH YOUR COLLEAGUES, THOSE ABOVE YOU AND BELOW YOU AS WELL AS THOSE WHO ARE AT YOUR LEVEL. Those who supervise you and those you supervise will elevate you to a higher position. Nobody will receive a management position unless he or she has someone to manage or unless someone has helped elevate him or her to a higher position.

- NETWORK WITH OTHER MANAGERS. During your career, you have an excellent chance of being terminated, fired, transferred, demoted, pushed out, downsized, or whatever else you want to call it. One day you are very happy with your work and the next day you are out. It happened to me one time. That was a low ebb in my life, but it only lasted for one week. During the previous fifteen years, I had done what is commonly known as networking. Because of my network, I avoided losing even a week's pay.

- KNOW WHO THE LEADERS ARE. My former pastor, Dr. Floyd Roebuck, suggested that secret to success. It's true whether you are a minister, a supervisor, a manager, or the president of the organization. Remember, the leader isn't necessarily the person in a certain position but the one who actually influences others.

- OVERCOME THE BAD THINGS THAT MAY HAPPEN. *Fired* is a negative word. I don't know anything tougher than looking for a new job. But, discouragement does not have to live with you forever if you have been fired for something other than dishonesty.

- BE RECEPTIVE TO RETRAINING. You must be receptive to being retrained and not get down on yourself. One of the best examples of this need occurred when the space budget was reduced and engineers by the thousands found themselves looking for work and needing to be retrained.

- USE THE SKILLS YOU HAVE, EVEN WHEN PEOPLE THINK YOU'RE OVERQUALIFIED FOR A GIVEN POSITION. I talked to a friend in Nashville, Tennessee, who had a master's degree in music. He needed a job. Several told him he was overqualified. He quickly told them his master's degree in music did not hurt his "picking."

- PUT SOMETHING BACK INTO THE COMMUNITY. Most managers I know are givers and not takers.

Be smart, not dumb, with your management decisions.

Part VI.

Watch Your Step Here

55

DOWNSIZING AND GREEDINESS

Downsizing seems to be a fact of life. Recently I read an article that sickened me. The article was about one of this country's major corporations with thousands of employees. For the past seventy-five years, this company has made a major contribution to our society.

Many of this company's current employees started work at entry-level jobs. These same people have invented products, designed products, built products, provided administration for the company, advertised the products, and sold the products.

Millions of Americans and people throughout the world have purchased the company's products. Management, employees, and stockholders alike have enjoyed the good life because of the fine work of these employees. Leadership has been evident from the bottom to the top of this company, and leadership from the top down has been an inspiration to our free enterprise system.

One day the stockholders looked around and saw they were not receiving the dividends they expected. They said to the board of directors, "Is this the best you can do?" The board said to the president, "Is this the best you can do?" The president repeated the same question to the vice president, the vice president to the manager, the manager to the supervisor, the supervisor to the employees. Each asked, "Is this the best you can do?"

The president said, "I can and will correct this dividend problem. I went to the best business school, and I've attended the best university on strategic planning. You want bottom-line increases. I know how to give you bottom-line increases and bigger dividends." He was positive and confident. The action taken by the president or corporate savior was so simple I believe a second semester business major in Economics 101 could have solved the problem for the short haul. He did what is now popularly known as "downsizing." He terminated, laid off, fired, and forced early retirement on 50,000 people.

You may assign whatever title to the action you like. The end result is the same.

The old saying is appropriate: "When your neighbor loses his job, it is a *recession,* but when you lose *your* job it is a *depression.*" The employees who kept their jobs must have had a feeling of relief that they survived the cut. Some must have thought it was because of their talent, education, hard work, company loyalty and special skill that saved their job. Probably most of that is true.

I'm sure that the annual report once again showed positive numbers in a way that it had not shown for a long time. The board room must have been one happy room by the end of the year. I suspect there were more giggles there than at the honeymoon suite at the local motel.

Can you imagine how the downsizer leader must have felt when the annual statement was reviewed by the board members? The board saw the fine letter that was drafted and would be mailed to all the stockholders. The board members would be first to hear the good news before the annual statement and letter was sent to the stockholders. I can hear the buttons popping off the board members' shirts as they made the motion for the "downsizer" to receive sixteen million dollars ($16,000,000) in his compensation package for the great work. The person to second the motion must have nearly reached the ceiling with hand outstretched to be sure the chair saw his or her hand. Also, to have the motion made, seconded, and then recorded in the minutes must have been a fine feeling. Then the other board members must have given a cheer for the hero of the hour. Some must have said the "downsizer" earned every dime of it.

Recently, I made a presentation to the Executive Round Table, which is a group of Berry College students and local business and industry leaders. I titled the presentation "Dumb Things Smart Managers Do." This board meeting could have been titled "Dumb Things Smart Boards Do." Did that board of directors make a good decision to vote one person sixteen million dollars ($16,000,000)? Did one person earn that much money?

What is the attitude of the people terminated? Many of the people terminated had helped build the company to be one of the biggest and finest in the world. What is the attitude of the people still working for the company? What is the attitude of the local communities where the good people worked? What is the public attitude? Does the public still have a positive attitude toward the company's president? The people left had to have a feeling of relief, and the stockholders must be elated with this new-found dividend wealth.

The plan to save this company plus hundreds across the country is sometimes absolutely necessary. My only recommendation would be for the stockholders to call a meeting and fire the board members who voted to pay the downsizer sixteen million dollars. Since the early days of this civilization, greed and gluttony have been behind many actions, but greed and gluttony have never been accepted as being in good taste in our society.

I can hear questions shouted from other board rooms, *Well, how much then? Why not pay this person sixteen million dollars?* The board might point out that one person in our country receives fifteen million each year for jumping up and down singing songs for two hours while wearing one glove. Another person receives thirty-two million dollars for wearing two gloves and hitting another person for three minutes.

Just a little common sense, however, tells us this logic is flawed. We do not pay five-star generals a million dollars a year to keep us free. Recently, when a would-be dictator needed to be stopped, we did not give sixteen million dollars to a five-star general and a four-star general to stop him, and neither did we give the many entry-level and middle management leaders in the military thousands of dollars to stop him.

Then how much should the board have given that company head? Answering that kind of question is why the board is on the 42nd floor. They are not there to make dumb decisions or to make one person so fat. Fat clogs the veins. What an opportunity that board of directors had to make a difference. Think of other decisions they could have made. They could have

- PUT THE EXCESS EARNINGS BACK IN THE COMPANY

- PAID THE EXTRA MONEY TO THE STOCKHOLDERS

- GIVEN HUNDREDS OF DESERVING EMPLOYEES A BONUS

- DEPOSITED EXTRA MONEY INTO EMPLOYEES' RETIREMENT OR PROFIT-SHARING PLANS

- GIVEN TO CHARITY

You might like to add to the list.

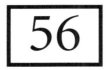

MAKING THE MOST OF A MERGER

In the last few years, it seems many of our smaller businesses have spent much of their time looking for the right merger or more often than not an outright sale. Many small-town banks, funeral homes, medical clinics, or other small businesses have merged or sold to the mega-corporation. Their owners made big bucks.

If you have a profitable small business and are considering selling it to a giant corporation, you'd do well to remember this version of the Golden Rule: "The one with the gold rules." The mega-corporation folks are not going to give you their money and still let you make the decisions.

For the small business owner, the merger or sell-out could be a great opportunity. You may want to take the money, enjoy the good life, and let someone else worry about the payroll, liability, lawsuits, strikes, taxes, customer complaints, competition, and worn-out equipment.

Too, if you are an entry-level employee or in management, you may also hit "pay dirt" in the merger. You could be pushed up the ladder. Senior management tends to do better with the severance pay, but mergers tend to help middle managers and entry-level employees with their jobs. The acquiring company management would rather have someone to do the work than to have advice or opinions from senior management or from owners whom they just paid a lot of cash or stock.

If the merger does not bring you some sort of buy-out or a better job, now might be the time for you to make the move and do something you always wanted to do. It could be time for you to form a business or company where you have an ownership position. My own observations and research revealed that those who have a sizable ownership or equity position move to a higher level economically in their own business. You will probably work harder and longer hours, but you will probably enjoy it more.

So, own the business if possible. If not, have as much of it as you can with stock and stock options. If it is a partnership, work to be a senior partner as soon as possible. If you are in management, make a special effort to be part of the decision-making group. Whether you are an entry-level employee or an employee with some seniority, be creative, be productive, and make the kind of contribution that will cause management and your co-workers to recognize and express your value to the company or organization.

57

Sometimes You Just Have to Take a Risk

When I was stationed at Fort Rucker, Alabama, many years ago, I met my bride-to-be one Sunday evening at First Baptist Church in Enterprise, Alabama. She was raised Methodist, but sometimes in the rural South a young Methodist girl or boy would drift astray and marry a Baptist. She had just been crowned Dale County Maid of Cotton. Not only did she look good, but her Mama was one of the South's best cooks. I also learned Carolyn had ranked really high herself in a 4-H cooking contest.

I knew pretty quickly that our meeting was a stroke of luck for me. It was not many months before my time with Uncle Sam would be ending. My family had left the farm in southeast Georgia and moved to Jacksonville, Florida. As the time drew near for my army time to end, I asked her whether she would like to spend the rest of her life with me. After some time, she said "Yes," and the last forty years have been really good, at least for me.

The risk was not very great for me, but maybe it was for her. I had accepted a job for $55 per week plus commission. The first year (1957), I earned $7,500. By today's standards that does not seem like much. However, our house payment including insurance and taxes was $45 per month—not bad then for a two-bedroom, one-bath home in a nice neighborhood. The doctor bill to deliver our son in 1958 was $150, and the hospital stay was three days at $12 per day. The doctor's fee for an appendectomy was $150, and gasoline was 21 cents per gallon.

The reason I mention these prices to you is to help you keep income and buying power in the proper perspective. Also, many managers who now make a lot of money remember how little they earned at their entry-level position. Many will want to work you for as little as possible. This mind-set is not based on reality but on their memory of how tough it was and how little they earned when they began. But they could buy a new car for less than $2,500. They should remember what a similar new car costs today—at least $16,000-$18,000.

Most parents know it is not best to give their children everything. They know it is good for them to struggle and have some tough times. They feel it builds character.

So you can tell the "Big Guy or Girl" behind the Big Desk that you have already had the character-building course. You are ready to be compensated at a high level for what you are doing. Tell the boss your productivity and your contribution are going to make a difference to him or her and to the company. All you want is an opportunity.

The Big Boss generally likes to hear this kind of conversation. If it is a closely-held organization where the top people are also doing most of the work, you are going to be exactly the person they are looking for. They are ready to slow down, they have fought all the battles they want to fight, and their interest is turning more towards their beach house, mountain home, or more time with their grandchildren.

If you find you can preserve and grow what they have spent their life building, you are in a great position to talk about "equity" in the not too distant future. Just do what you say you will do, and do it now.

So, look for the opportunity and prepare for the opportunity. Then take the risk in your personal life and in your career. Don't compromise your integrity, of course. Remember, too, that usually the greater the risk, the greater the reward.

58

THE POWER OR THE PROBLEM OF TOUCH

Some families are touchers and huggers, and some families never touch or hug. Some are kissers, and some are not. I am not big on the kissers, but most of my family—both men and women—are huggers.

Many folks in our society never talk much about their feelings. It's sad, but many boys were told that big boys don't cry. The other day I was reminded of this while watching a movie about the life of Alvin York, from the great state of Tennessee. Alvin York was the most decorated soldier of World War I. He did not want to go to war. He did not believe in killing other people. However, when he understood that his fighting would protect the people he loved, he was willing to join the fight.

In the movie, as Alvin boarded the train, he hugged his mother, brother, and sister. Then he hugged his girlfriend. His minister, to whom he was quite close, was also present to see him off. Alvin shook his minister's hand and boarded the train. Back then, "big boys" and men did not hug.

When the war was over, the French government honored Alvin York before he returned to America to be honored by millions. The French general marched up to Sergeant York, who was standing at attention. The general pinned a medal on his chest and kissed him on each cheek. The camera zoomed in on Sergeant York's eyes as they said, "I'm just not believing this." I'm sure some of his buddies explained this custom to him.

Not long ago, I attended a meeting where the speaker told of lawsuits that cost companies millions of dollars because a person touched or hugged another person who did not want to be hugged or touched. The next week when I returned to the office, I went out of the touching and hugging business. Some of this is sad, because I have worked closely for many years with some co-workers who are also good friends. You would think most would know what good office manners are. Since you might have one person from a hugging family and one from a non-hugging family, though, it could cost the company lots of money and you a demotion, transfer, or termination. So, save your hugging for someplace other than with your co-workers.

Not long ago I was attending a marketing meeting in Orlando, Florida. One of the speakers was a psychologist who was a specialist in human behavior and what makes a person tick. He really had my attention and the attention of everyone in the meeting.

The speaker did about an hour on the importance of touching and hugging. He said we needed one good hug in the morning and one good hug in the evening for good mental health. He indicated several more hugs during the day would make us an even better person.

Our assignment during the break was to hug three people we did not know. When the break time came it was like greeting time at my church. You never saw such hugging. I wanted to pick the three best candidates to complete the assignment. A couple of the attendees looked like Miss Central Florida. The doors were open, and you never saw so many people completing this assignment. I hugged two beautiful women who were wearing "Now and Forever" perfume. I thought, this is not a bad assignment.

I turned around, and a big 6'4" man was standing there. He looked like a second-string tackle with the Atlanta Falcons. I grabbed him and said, "Are you into all this hugging?"

He said, "Not until now."

In just a second I noticed he did not have on the name tag for our meeting. He said he wasn't part of our meeting, but he had just stopped by to see what was going on. After that I went out of the hugging business for sure.

A hug is often an excellent way to express deep feelings. But if done improperly in the workplace, it could cost you your job and the company a big lawsuit.

So be careful in the workplace, but do not discount the importance of a hug. The best job in our town on the day of the children's Special Olympics is as one of the Official Huggers at the end of each race. Ask to be part of this special event in your town and you will always remember the power of touch. What does this have to do with getting a raise or promotion without asking? Everything. It imprints on your memory what is truly important in life.

59

SHATTERED LOVE COULD SHATTER FINANCIAL PLANS

People promise to marry "for better or for worse, for richer or for poorer, in sickness and in health." These vows, if kept, can and will have a great impact on your health and wealth.

The beginning point is this. Try to be as sure as possible before you take the vows. If there is one thing about your mate-to-be that you cannot stand, but you think your love is so great you take the vows believing you can change that person, forget it. Cut your losses, and get out of the relationship. You have less chance of changing the person than Aunt Lucy has of hitting the $20 million lottery.

Divorce costs. Not counting the personal hurt, there have been greater financial losses because couples marry, have families, and then divorce, than almost any other cause. We can talk about training, education, pay raises, and promotions until Wednesday, but if you don't keep your personal life right, you are not going to do well with your finances. You might give the example of some relative who went through four divorces and still received big promotions and made millions. Only on rare occasions does that happen, however.

Related to the situation of "shattered love," the idea of having a happy spouse at home and someone else across town and no one being hurt is ridiculous. If you play, you will pay. The price, both financially and otherwise, is steep.

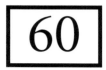

What About Your Personal Financial Plan?

If you have worked hard, planned well, and made a great contribution to your company or organization, you are to be commended and congratulated. Accept all the accolades with a high degree of pride. You have provided a good standard of living for yourself and your family, and you also have contributed to the well-being of your colleagues.

But have you thought of everything? You need to think about these things, too:

- DO YOU HAVE A WILL? EVERYONE DOES—YOURS OR THE STATE'S. (SEE THE APPENDIX, "LAST WILL AND TESTAMENT," FOR THE VERSION THAT EXISTS IN MANY STATES.)

- IS YOUR WILL UP-TO-DATE?

- DO YOU KNOW HOW AN ESTATE WILL SHRINK WITHOUT PROPER PLANNING? (SEE "ESTATES OF FAMOUS PERSONS" IN THE APPENDIX.)

- DO YOU KNOW ABOUT TRUSTS AND HOW THEY WILL HELP CONSERVE YOUR ESTATE?

- DO YOU HAVE LIFE INSURANCE? HOW MUCH? FOR WHAT PURPOSE? HERE ARE A FEW NEEDS THAT LIFE INSURANCE SHOULD MEET: (1) FINAL EXPENSES—BURIAL, MEDICAL, AND UNPAID BILLS; (2) COLLEGE FUND FOR THE CHILDREN; (3) CASH TO PAY THE REMAINDER OF THE MORTGAGE; (4) CASH FOR EMERGENCY FUND, RETIREMENT, OR OTHER USE; (5) CASH TO PAY COURT COSTS, ATTORNEY FEES, CPA FEES, AND ESTATE TAXES.

- DO YOU HAVE DISABILITY INCOME INSURANCE?

Here are some of the people who can help you with your financial plan:

- YOUR CPA

- YOUR LIFE INSURANCE AGENT

- YOUR BANKER

- YOUR FINANCIAL PLANNER

- YOUR STOCKBROKER

- YOUR MUTUAL FUND ADVISOR

- YOUR ATTORNEY

Some companies or organizations offer the services of many of these professionals to assist you. If you are preparing your own plan, a few questions to any of them will give you suggestions about whom to select. Most will be in your own community.

If you have had your attention devoted to the efforts of the company, now might be a good time to have a personal checkup of your own personal financial plan. These are just a few questions to help you think of your own personal financial plan or goal:

- WHAT ABOUT SOCIAL SECURITY? YOUR LOCAL SOCIAL SECURITY OFFICE OR ANY OF THE PEOPLE JUST MENTIONED CAN HELP YOU GET AN UPDATE ON YOUR FUTURE SOCIAL SECURITY BENEFITS.

- WHAT ABOUT YOUR COMPANY RETIREMENT PLAN?

- DOES YOUR COMPANY HAVE A 401(K) PLAN?

- FOR THE SELF-EMPLOYED, DO YOU HAVE A KEOGH PLAN?

- ARE YOU SAVING ALL THE TAX DOLLARS YOU CAN OR JUST PAYING AND COMPLAINING?

- DOES YOUR COMPANY HAVE A PROFIT SHARING PLAN? IF NOT, SUGGEST ONE.

- WHAT ARE THE FINANCIAL ADVANTAGES OF WORKING TO OR PAST AGE 70?

I hope that at the end of your work career, you will have "made it big." It does not much matter how big. If you have enjoyed the journey, that's what really matters.

Decide now to whom you will leave your "empire," even if it is ever so small. Most of us will take care of our family first and then think of others. Here are some other possibilities:

- YOUR CHURCH

- YOUR FAVORITE COLLEGE OR UNIVERSITY

- BOYS OR GIRLS CLUB

- THE RED CROSS

- THE SALVATION ARMY

- THE CANCER SOCIETY

- THE CURE FOR LUNG DISEASE

- THE CURE OF DIABETES

- SOMETHING FOR THE ENVIRONMENT

- THE NATIONAL DEBT

I'm sure I have left off one or two of your favorites.

Just remember: Although getting raises and promotions is important, it's also important to make the most of what you make.

APPENDIX A.

ESTATES OF FAMOUS PERSONS

Name	Gross Estate	Total Settlement Costs	Net Estate	Percent Shrinkage
Stan Laurel	91,562	8,381	83,181	9%
William Frawley	92,446	45,814	46,632	49%
"Gabby" Hayes	111,327	21,963	89,364	20%
Hedda Hopper	472,661	165,982	306,679	35%
Nelson Eddy	472,715	109,990	362,725	23%
Marilyn Monroe	819,176	448,750	370,426	55%
W. C. Fields	884,680	329,793	554,887	37%
Humphrey Bogart	910,146	274,234	635,912	30%
Dixie Crosby	1,332,571	781,953	550,618	59%
E. Stanley Gardner	1,795,092	636,705	1,158,387	35%
F. D. Roosevelt	1,940,999	574,867	1,366,132	30%
Clark Gable	2,806,526	1,101,038	1,705,488	30%
Cecil B. DeMille	4,043,607	1,396,064	2,647,543	35%
Al Jolson	4,385,143	1,349,066	3,036,077	31%
Gary Cooper	4,984,985	1,530,454	3,454,531	31%
Henry Kaiser, Sr.	5,597,772	2,488,364	3,109,408	44%
Harry M. Warner	8,946,618	2,308,444	6,638,174	26%
Elvis Presley	10,165,434	7,374,635	2,790,799	73%
Alwin C. Ernst, cpa	12,642,431	7,124,112	5,518,319	56%
J. P. Morgan	17,121,482	11,893,691	5,227,791	69%
William E. Boeing	22,386,158	10,589,748	11,796,410	47%
Walt Disney	23,004,851	6,811,943	16,192,908	30%
J.D.Rockefeller I	26,905,182	17,124,988	9,780,194	64%
F. Vanderbilt	76,838,530	42,846,112	33,992,418	56%

APPENDIX B.

LAST WILL AND TESTAMENT (STATE VERSION)

Is this the will you'd really like to use? It contains provisions your state may use if you don't make a will yourself.

BEING OF SOUND MIND AND MEMORY, I DO HEREBY AGREE FOR THIS DOCUMENT TO BE USED AS MY LAST WILL AND TESTAMENT.

FIRST, ALTHOUGH MY SURVIVING SPOUSE WILL NEED ALL OF THE FINANCIAL HELP POSSIBLE, I GIVE MY SPOUSE ONLY ONE-HALF OF MY POSSESSIONS. I GIVE MY CHILDREN THE REMAINING HALF.

SECOND, I APPOINT MY SURVIVING SPOUSE AS GUARDIAN OF OUR CHILDREN. IN SPITE OF MY UTMOST CONFIDENCE IN MY SPOUSE'S JUDGMENT, HOWEVER, I REQUIRE THAT A REPORT BE GIVEN TO THE PROBATE COURT EACH AND EVERY YEAR TO ACCOUNT FOR HOW, WHY, AND WHERE THE MONEY WAS SPENT FOR PROPER CARE OF THE CHILDREN. FURTHER, IN SPITE OF MY UTMOST CONFIDENCE IN MY SPOUSE'S INTEGRITY, I DIRECT THAT MY SPOUSE TAKE THE NECESSARY TIME AND MONEY TO OBTAIN A PERFORMANCE BOND TO GUARANTEE TO THE PROBATE COURT THAT PROPER JUDGMENT WILL BE EXERCISED IN HANDLING, INVESTING, AND SPENDING THE CHILDREN'S MONEY. AS A FINAL SAFEGUARD, IN SPITE OF MY DESIRE TO FREE MY SURVIVING SPOUSE FROM UNDUE BURDENS, I GIVE OUR CHILDREN, WHEN THEY BECOME OF LEGAL AGE, THE RIGHT TO DEMAND AND RECEIVE

A COMPLETE ACCOUNTING OF ALL FINANCIAL ACTIONS TAKEN WITH OUR MONEY.

THIRD, SHOULD MY SPOUSE REMARRY AND SUBSEQUENTLY DIE HAVING MADE NO WILL, THE NEW SPOUSE SHALL BE ENTITLED TO ONE-HALF OF EVERYTHING MY SPOUSE POSSESSED. SHOULD MY CHILDREN NEED SOME OF THIS SHARE FOR FOOD, CLOTHES, OR OTHER SUPPORT, THE NEW SPOUSE MAY LEGALLY REFUSE TO SPEND ANY OF IT ON THEIR BEHALF. FURTHERMORE, AT MY SPOUSE'S DEATH, THE SECOND SPOUSE SHALL ALSO HAVE SOLE RIGHT TO DECIDE WHO IS TO GET THIS SHARE; MY CHILDREN MAY LEGALLY BE EXCLUDED.

FOURTH, SHOULD MY SPOUSE PREDECEASE ME OR DIE WHILE ANY OF OUR CHILDREN ARE MINORS, I DO NOT WISH TO EXERCISE MY RIGHT TO NOMINATE THE GUARDIAN OF OUR CHILDREN. RATHER, I DIRECT MY RELATIVES AND FRIENDS TO GET TOGETHER AND ARGUE ABOUT IT. IF THEY FAIL TO AGREE ON A GUARDIAN, I DIRECT THE PROBATE COURT TO MAKE THE SELECTION. IF THE COURT WANTS TO APPOINT A COMPLETE STRANGER, THAT WILL BE FINE.

FIFTH, ALTHOUGH UNDER EXISTING LAW THERE ARE CERTAIN LEGAL WAYS TO LOWER THE AMOUNT OF FEDERAL ESTATE TAXES PAYABLE AT MY DEATH AND ALTHOUGH MY SPOUSE AND CHILDREN COULD PUT THIS MONEY TO GOOD USE, I WOULD RATHER GIVE THE MONEY TO THE INTERNAL REVENUE SERVICE.

IN WITNESS WHEREOF, I HAVE SET MY HAND TO THIS LAST WILL AND TESTAMENT EVEN THOUGH MY SIGNATURE MAY BE UNNECESSARY FOR IT TO BE IN EFFECT.[1]

---

[1]Adapted from an unknown source.

APPENDIX C.

THE RULE OF 72

The "rule of 72" provides a way of determining when money will double. The formula for the "rule of 72" is to divide 72 by the amount of interest. So, your money will double

- IN 24 YEARS AT 3% INTEREST

- IN 12 YEARS AT 6% INTEREST

- IN 8 YEARS AT 9% INTEREST

- IN 6 YEARS AT 12% INTEREST

- IN 4 YEARS AND 10 MONTHS AT 15% INTEREST

Three secrets to making the most of what you make are to (1) get an excellent rate of return, (2) have time on your side, and (3) keep saving every month.

APPENDIX D.

HOW MUCH INSURANCE DO YOU NEED?

Life Insurance

If you are paying for life insurance, the premium always seems to be too much. If you are the beneficiary, "too much" does not seem to be enough.

If you are buying to protect your family, you should buy five to eight times your annual income. Business partners should have enough life insurance on each other to purchase the partner's share of the business from his or her heirs. If your corporation is redeeming stock, the corporation should have enough life insurance on your life to buy your stock. If you need cash to pay estate taxes, your CPA can give you a projection of how much you will need.

You may have other assets that will take care of all of these needs. If so, you can decide whether the purchase of life insurance in each case is your best option.

What kind of life insurance should you buy? Basically, there are three kinds of life insurance. Permanent life insurance builds cash value and requires a higher premium. It's like buying versus renting a home. Term life insurance is like renting and has a lower premium. Permanent/term is a mixture of the two. Other kinds of life insurance include universal life, which provides the insured the option of determining how much he or she wants to pay for insurance and for what period of time. A type of insurance that has become popular is variable life, in which the insured is covered by life insurance and also has the option of selecting one of several mutual funds as part of the package.

If you know you will die soon, buy term life insurance. If you are not quite sure when you will die, then buy as much permanent insurance as you need and can afford. If you feel good about the stock market, then buy as much variable universal life as you can afford.

Health Insurance

A good major medical or other health plan offered by your employer is usually your best buy. If you are self-employed, your best buy will usually be a major medical plan from an insurance company or other health provider.

The best way to receive a lower premium is to buy a plan with the largest deductible you can afford. Ask your insurance agent to give you a printout of your premiums with deductibles of $250, $500, and $1,000, and you will get a good idea of your savings.

Long-Term Care

As we go into the twenty-first century, many people are taking a close look at long-term care. If you are within a few years of your retirement, you would do well to take a good look at long-term care. If you have parents for whom a long-term illness would wipe out their resources (and your inheritance), you might suggest long-term care to them. We no longer live in a society where our parents and grandparents will spend their last fifteen years living with their children.

Auto Insurance

The best way to save money on your auto insurance is once again to buy as large a deductible plan as you can afford. Even better than the deductible is to slow down and not get so many speeding tickets. Also, call your auto insurance agent before you buy your next automobile. The agent can tell you which cars are most likely to be stolen. Too, if you feel you just have to drink and drive, take a sober driver with you.

Homeowner Insurance

Buying a policy with a large deductible is also a way to save money on your homeowner insurance. For additional savings, buy smoke detectors and live near a fire station and water hydrant.

APPENDIX E.

USING CREDIT WISELY

Here are a few tips to help you use credit wisely.

- BUILD A GOOD RELATIONSHIP WITH THE BANKER. IF YOU ARE SAVING OR BORROWING, ONE OR TWO PERCENT CAN MAKE A BIG DIFFERENCE.

- KNOW THE DIFFERENCE BETWEEN GOOD DEBT AND BAD DEBT. GOOD DEBT INCLUDES SUCH THINGS AS HOME MORTGAGES OR SELF-FINANCED LOANS. BAD DEBT INCLUDES HIGH-INTEREST CREDIT CARDS AND AUTOMOBILE LOANS.

- BORROW FOR THE SHORTEST PERIOD AT THE LOWEST INTEREST.

- BORROW ONLY WHAT YOU CAN AFFORD.

- MAKE THE PAYMENT WHEN IT IS DUE. YOU'LL AVOID PAYING LATE CHARGES AND WILL ALSO MAINTAIN A GOOD CREDIT RATING. IN THE LONG RUN, IT'S BETTER TO MAINTAIN A GOOD REPUTATION THAN TO TRY TO USE THE "GRACE PERIOD" TO MAKE A FEW EXTRA PENNIES.

- MAKE AN EXTRA MORTGAGE PAYMENT AS OFTEN AS YOU CAN.

About the Author

Earl Tillman is an insurance executive and speaker. Earl lives in Rome, Georgia, where he is vice president of State Mutual Insurance Company. He speaks to groups all over the country and would be glad to speak to your group. Write him at the address on page 154 or call him at 706-235-9840 (toll-free 1-888-235-9840). His e-mail address is 70420.3714@compuserve.com.

Earl and his wife Carolyn have two children and three grandchildren.

An Easy Way to Get More Copies of This Book

For additional copies of *How to Get a Raise or Promotion Without Asking,* mail your check for $19.95 plus $3.00 shipping and handling ($22.95 total for each book) to the following address:

Wealth Communications
26 Saddle Mountain Road
Rome, Georgia 30161

Recommendation

"Earl Tillman knows what he's talking about because he's done it. People who read this book and put its principles into practice will learn how to make a life as well as a living, and they'll be happier while they're doing it."

—Dr. Ross West, author, *Go to Work and Take Your Faith Too!* and *How to Be Happier in the Job You Sometimes Can't Stand,* Rome, Georgia